SUCCESS WITH

BAMBOOS & ORNAMENTAL GRASSES

Lucinda Costello

GUILD OF MASTER CRAFTSMAN
PUBLICATIONS LTD

First published 2008 by
Guild of Master Craftsman Publications Ltd
Castle Place, 166 High Street
Lewes, East Sussex BN7 1XU

All the pictures were taken by the author, except for those listed below:
Morguefile.com: p15 (bottom right), p93 (top left); Christopher Bibb: p93 (bottom left).

ISBN: 978-1-86108-479-8

A catalogue record for this book is available from the British Library.

Associate Publisher: Jonathan Bailey
Production Manager: Jim Bulley
Managing Editor: Gerrie Purcell
Editor: Rachel Netherwood
Managing Art Editor: Gilda Pacitti
Designer: John Hawkins

Set in Futura
Colour origination by GMC Reprographics
Printed and bound in Singapore by Kyodo Printing

SUCCESS WITH
BAMBOOS &
ORNAMENTAL
GRASSES

Contents

LEFT **In this quirky planting at Knoll Gardens, Dorset,**
Hakonechloa macra **'Aureola' forms a graceful mound**
encircling a cherry tree

Introduction

Over the past few years we've seen an incredible upsurge in the popularity of grasses and bamboos as ornamental garden plants.

Now, more than ever, this exciting group of plants is being allowed to step forward and take an increasingly important role in our gardens. Gardeners are becoming bolder with their selections and using grasses and bamboos to paint swathes of texture through their borders. And with this new-found popularity dawns a revelation to soothe those nagging fears – the majority of ornamental specimens will not run amuck or thuggishly smother your garden!

To clarify matters before we go any further, bamboos are in fact a member of the grass family but are often singled out as a stand-alone group. This is because they are the only division to form woody stems, giving them a very distinctive look indeed.

Just as on the catwalk, garden trends come and go, but readers with a penchant for garden history will know that grasses and bamboos have been smouldering away in fashionable circles for many a gardener's year. And this is because, as well as being beautiful, they're so very versatile. There really is a grass for every garden situation. *Carex elata* 'Aurea' and *Cyperus papyrus* will revel in the moisture of a pond margin; *Miscanthus sinensis* and *Panicum virgatum* will lap up full sun on dryish ground; and *Luzula sylvatica* 'Aurea' will brighten up a tricky spot in dry shade.

If you haven't got much space to call a garden, fear not. As long as you're willing to be attentive with watering when it's needed, grasses and bamboos make great potted specimens. They look especially interesting when arranged in groups of contrasting foliage colours and habits. And in fact, bamboos that you deem too vigorous for the garden can still be enjoyed if confined to a large container. Take the graceful, distinctive *Chimonobambusa tumidissinoda* for example. With its slender stems, very prominently swollen at the nodes, and its arching fans of narrow foliage, who wouldn't want this bamboo in their garden? It's simply perfect growing along a pathway or where the reflection of its elegant form can be caught in a pool. Problem is it can spread to around 26ft (8m) in optimum conditions! A glorious spectacle no doubt, but sadly not something that many of us gardeners can accommodate on our plots. So put it in a big pot and you'll enjoy all the good bits whilst restricting height and of course spread.

Grass aficionados will be horrified but it's true that some gardeners think grasses are a bit boring; that their border space would be better filled with something a bit more showy. Well, if this is you, I strongly encourage you to think again. Grasses can make a dramatic statement on their own, particularly when planted in groups. And when combined with flowering perennials, grasses make a perfect foil, stepping into the limelight as summer turns to autumn and their flower plumes burst forth to sparkle in the soft golden light.

So read on and discover that whatever your favoured planting style, be it cottage or contemporary, coastal or containerized, grasses and bamboos can bring texture, movement and year-round drama. Once you fall for their charms you'll be hooked!

OPPOSITE **Semiarundinaria fastuosa** is an impressive, vigorous bamboo tolerant of a wide range of conditions

LEFT Bamboo canes are used throughout the world for everything from cooking utensils to building materials

CHAPTER 1

An introduction to grasses & bamboos

Bamboos and grasses have been muscling their way into planting schemes for many years now. Championed by some and simply dismissed as show pieces by others, their journey into popular planting hasn't always been easy. But these days, thanks to nurserymen and garden designers around the globe, we are being spoiled for choice when it comes to exciting new varieties and hard-to-come-by rarities.

GRASSES AND BAMBOOS IN DESIGN

Grasses have been championed most recently by the likes of Dutch designer Piet Oudolf, with his wonderful prairie planting; English plantsman Neil Lucas, with his inspiring Dorset grass garden; and Washington-based designers Wolfgang Oehme and James van Sweden. The latter have developed their own way of planting that they call 'New American Garden Style'. Based on the native American prairies, their style

ABOVE Many contemporary designers take inspiration from the prairies of North America. This border at Knoll Gardens in Dorset, seen here early one August morning, is a wonderful example of naturalistic-style planting

relies heavily on grasses. James van Sweden's words express the new freedom that gardeners are enjoying: 'Do gardens have to be so tame, so harnessed, so unfree? Our New American Garden is vigorous and audacious, and it vividly blends the natural and the cultivated.'

SLOW TO CATCH ON?

In the East, where bamboo grows as a native, gardeners realized its ornamental potential long before it was accepted by Western gardeners. During the 1800s, a few pioneering Western gardeners, designers and plantspeople knew that grasses and bamboos could create a storm and they were determined to show their contemporaries that it was time to start including them in planting schemes. Wealthy, fashion-conscious Victorian gardeners developed a fascination with plants from far-flung corners of the globe. Not quite as extreme, but reminiscent of the Dutch 'tulip fever' of the seventeenth century, landowners began to see palms, bamboos and other exotics as must-have fashion accessories. They had become tired of their English gardens that only held interest for a few months of the year, and mysterious plants such as bamboo and pampas grass gained them status in fashionable circles. Bamboo was seen as a tender curiosity until Lord de Saumarez proved a certain species hardy in his garden at Shrubland Hall in Suffolk.

But it all got a bit much, gardens had become something of a novelty, a trophy of wealth. William Robinson, the influential gardener and writer of the Arts and Crafts movement, was all for the use of grasses and bamboos as long as they were included in a tasteful way. He called for a return to traditional English gardens in a style he described as 'the wild garden'. From this developed the English cottage garden style that we still know and embrace today.

William Robinson and Gertrude Jekyll became firm friends and certainly influenced each other's work. In 1908 Gertrude Jekyll

ABOVE **Bamboo grows wild in the forests of Thailand, Japan, China and other Eastern countries. It gained recognition as a garden-worthy plant in this area long before its acceptance in the West**

designed a 4½ acre garden at Upton Grey in Hampshire. Part of the plot was laid down as a wild garden and several bamboos were planted, including *Pleioblastus simonii* and *Pseudosasa japonica*. If Gertrude could plant them, they must be all right!

At the time, the direction that gardening should be taking provoked heated debate between the prominent garden designers of the era, including William Robinson and Reginald Blomfeld.

NATIONAL COLLECTION OF BAMBOO

A little less confrontational in his approach, but still as sure of the ornamental merits of bamboos, in 1891 Sir William Thiselton-Dyer created the Bamboo Garden at the Royal Botanic Gardens Kew, during his directorship (1885–1905). This important garden continues to thrive and develop, testament to Sir William's vision. It currently holds the UK's largest collection of bamboos with more than 130 varieties.

GRASSES AND BAMBOOS AROUND THE WORLD

Grasses can be found everywhere. They grow outside our windows and on patches of wasteland, up mountains and in fields, forests, meadows and bogs. We eat them, sit on them, wear them and we extract power from them. But their fabulous ornamental qualities mean that they have long been recognized for their positive contribution in the cultivated garden setting.

ABOVE **Wild grasses can be just as beautiful as cultivated ones**

ABOVE **If you're still not sure about grasses try mixing them with herbaceous perennials. Here** *Stipa gigantea* **creates wonderful movement amongst an otherwise fairly rigid planting**

WHY GROW BAMBOOS AND GRASSES?

Grasses grow all over the world, often in adverse conditions, and this has given rise to a host of qualities that make them resilient, gardenworthy plants. Bamboos, simply woody-stemmed grasses, grow wild on every continent except Europe. Now that bamboos have been truly embraced by the gardening community as beautiful, versatile plants, they have become widely available. Their elegant forms and diverse habits mean that there is a bamboo for every situation. Bamboos and grasses will grow in pots, form screens, give winter interest, provide ground cover; some grasses will even grow in water.

Some gardeners still shun grasses and these unfortunate ones seem to fall into two groups – those who like to impose strict order in the garden and think that grasses are untidy, unruly and will self-seed uncontrollably; and those (often really passionate gardeners) who would rather fill their borders with brightly coloured blooms, who feel that grasses are a waste of planting space. Well, as you will see on your journey through this book, there are indeed some fearsome grasses that will tower as tall as a house or spread to form a sea of heaving, swaying, whispering stems. But these are in the vast minority. Even if you stumble into the nursery and blindly select the first ornamental grass you lay your hands on, chances are that it will be a neat, clump-forming specimen with vibrant foliage and the promise of eye-catching, sparkler-like flower panicles.

Even if the undeniably wonderful blooms of herbaceous perennials have you hooked like a drug, grasses will only serve to intensify the heady feelings that plants can invoke. Consider the effect a bold ribbon of silky miscanthus flowerheads will have on your border as it weaves between your delphiniums, echinaceas, veronicas and astilbes, swaying rhythmically on the breeze.

ABOVE **Bamboo is globally important – here it's even being used as scaffolding to carry out repairs at the Grand Palace in Bangkok!**

ABOVE **Here on the River Kwai, and on rivers all over the Eastern world, bamboo houserafts are a common sight**

A GLOBAL ESSENTIAL

Grasses are one of the world's most important resources. Two-thirds of the calories and half the protein consumed globally come from grass crops – maize, wheat and rice. And it doesn't stop there. Where would we be without sugar, pasta, sweetcorn, cornflakes, beer and whisky? Grasses are used in tyres, sewage treatment, explosives and perfume.

Exciting research is now under way to extract clean, renewable energy from gardeners' favourite miscanthus. In fact this sustainable energy is already in use in some parts of the world. *Miscanthus x giganteus* puts on growth so rapidly that it can produce a staggering amount of burnable dry matter – who knows, one day in the future we may be filling up at the grass station!

In countries where bamboo grows wild and plentifully it is one of the most essential materials in everyday life. In China, Thailand, India, Nepal, Japan and many other countries, scaffolding, cooking utensils, homes, bridges, furniture and many more everyday objects are hewn from these strong, flexible stems.

So now we have acknowledged that grasses and bamboos are both ecologically and economically essential, let's get down to the important stuff – gardening!

ABOVE **Rice accounts for almost a quarter of all calories consumed by humans around the world. Paddy fields must be flooded to satisfy moisture-loving *Orzya sativa* and *O. glaberrima***

BACKGROUND

There are over 10,000 different grass species in the world. Add to that all the hybrids, subspecies, varieties, forms and cultivars, and you have a group of plants almost too numerous to imagine.

True grasses, bamboos, rushes, sedges, bullrushes and restios are all classed as grasses. Because true grasses, rushes and sedges have a similar appearance they are usually simply referred to as 'grasses'. Until fairly recently, curiously, the mainstream gardening community took little notice of restios. But now they've fallen very much into favour and they, like bamboos, are being singled out thanks to their different looks. Sometimes fern-like, sometimes reed-like, always quietly provocative, restios have a raw, prehistoric look about them that is found rarely in the popular, highly cultivated sector of the gardening world.

As for bamboos, it's patently obvious why they stand alone. Their hard, woody stems, often towering to dizzy heights, set them apart from any other grass.

ABOVE **Sempervivums are in the same family as...**

ABOVE **...rodgersias but they certainly look very different**

ONE BIG, HAPPY FAMILY

Grasses, rushes, sedges, restios and cat-tails are all families of grass. True grasses, including bamboos, are in the family Poaceae; rushes – Juncaceae; sedges – Cyperaceae; restios – Restionaceae; and cat-tails are in the family Typhaceae. Bamboos may be classed as grasses, but just as a rodgersia is wildly different in appearance to a saxifrage, despite being in the same family (Saxifragaceae), so a phyllostachys has seemingly little in common with a calamagrostis. The key to their similarities and differences lies in their family tree.

ABOVE **Because of their statuesque appearance you could be forgiven for not realizing that bamboos are actually grasses**

SIMPLE IS BEST

To keep things streamlined throughout this book true grasses, rushes, sedges, cat-tails and restios will be referred to as grasses. Bamboos will be referred to as bamboos.

MAKING SENSE OF BOTANICAL NAMES

The grass *Miscanthus sinensis* var. *condensatus* 'Cosmopolitan' is a member of the Poaceae family, as all grasses are. This is what all those names mean:

Poaceae – Family
Miscanthus – Genus
sinensis – Species
var. *condensatus* – Variety
'Cosmopolitan' – Cultivar

The correct naming of plants is known as botanical nomenclature and it gives us a single name by which a plant can be identified wherever in the world it grows. If you ever see ICBN, it means International Code of Botanical Nomenclature.

Botanical names are in Latin and are written as follows:

- Genus, species, variety, subspecies and forma should always be italicized.
- Genus should be written with a capital letter; species, variety, subspecies or forma are lower case.

- The abbreviations used to indicate variety, subspecies and forma should be in Roman script – var., subsp. and f.
- In a body of work where a plant has been named in full, such as *Miscanthus sinensis* var. *condensatus*, subsequent references may be abbreviated. The genus is reduced to its initial letter but species and so on should remain in full, e.g. *M. sinensis* var. *condensatus*.
- Cultivar names have capital letters and are written in Roman script. They are enclosed by single quotation marks, e.g. *M. sinensis* var. *condensatus* 'Cosmopolitan'.

You will note that during the course of this book I often use the term 'variety' when speaking of a particular plant. In this context I'm using the word in its literal sense rather than referring to a plant's botanical status. If a plant is in fact a botanical variety, the abbreviation 'var.' will always be included in its name.

ABOVE *Miscanthus sinensis* var. *condensatus* 'Cosmopolitan' may be a mouthful but it's a stunning plant that is certainly worth remembering

THOROUGHLY CHARMING OR TOTALLY CONFUSING?

ABOVE **Panicum is known by a dizzying array of common names**

I have used botanical names throughout this book to refer to specific plants. Any inclusion of common or vernacular names is purely for interest and is accompanied by the Latin name. A great deal of ambiguity arises from the use of common names and leads to confusing, misleading and often downright incorrect information. Charming they may be, but common names are often regional and new variations seem to spring up from nowhere. A plant has only one botanical name, no matter where in the world you find it. Take panicum for example; it's known as switchgrass, kleingrass, roundseed, vine mesquite, redtop and several other delightful but unhelpful common names. 'What a grouch!' I hear you say, but I assume that you prefer to know exactly which grass or bamboo you're purchasing, especially if you've spent time locating a particular variety. So at the risk of sounding like a bit of a misery, use the Latin name to avoid ambiguity.

ABOVE **The mottled young culms of *Chimonobambusa marmorea* are to be expected, thanks to its name**

WHAT'S IN A NAME?

Bamboos and grasses, like all plants, give away something of their heritage, appearance, properties, preferences or native habitat in their name. Take the example I've already used – *Miscanthus sinensis*; sinensis means from or native to China, just as *Pseudosasa japonica* originates in Japan. In fact you can read further into *P. japonica*'s name to deduce that it resembles a bamboo in the genus sasa – the prefix 'pseudo' means 'apparently but not actually'. Whilst understanding the Latin name of a plant is by no means essential, it's quite a fun skill to hone. For example, if you bought a lovely *Calamagrostis* x *acutiflora* 'Karl Foerster' in the spring, you'd know that you had some exciting flower spikes to look forward to – the prefix 'acuti' means spiky or pointed. Or maybe if a fine specimen of *Chimonobambusa marmorea* caught your eye, you'd know that some part of the plant was mottled (marmorea). As it happens, it's the beautifully slender, erect, emerging culms you need to watch out for.

Understanding a smattering of botanical Latin will also help you to work out a few facts about the plant in question. So if you'd like to grow *Leymus arenarius* then it would be useful to know that it needs a sandy, free-draining spot – arenarius relates to sandy places.

19

PHYSIOLOGY AND TERMINOLOGY

As with any plant, there are words used to describe the stems, leaves, flowers, roots and other 'body parts' of grasses and bamboos. These words become essential tools in the identification of a genus, and the species, forms, varieties and cultivars within it.

A flower or group of flowers held on a stem is known as an **inflorescence**. Grasses and bamboos don't need to have showy blooms to attract bees and other insects because they are pollinated thanks to the wind. The flowers of grasses are tiny and the impact they give as they glow in the autumn light is due to the massing of hundreds or thousands of individual blooms.

Throughout the plant world there are a number of different inflorescence arrangements. But the blooms of grasses and bamboos fall into one of the following compositions: **spike**, **raceme** or **panicle**. The stems of grasses and bamboos are called **culms** (although bamboo stems are commonly referred to as **canes**) and

the point at which a **leaf sheath** joins a stem is a **node**. The space between nodes is the **internode**; this measurement is useful when distinguishing similar species. The main part of the leaf, which blows around so enticingly in the breeze, is called the **blade**.

The roots of grasses and bamboos stretch far and wide, some reaching deeper than those of fully grown trees. In terms of growth habits, bamboos and grasses fall into two groups and it all comes down to their root systems. There are either **clump-formers** (**pachymorph** when referring to bamboo) or **runners** (**leptomorph** for bamboo). A swollen root that grows laterally underground is called a **rhizome** and these are also storage organs. A root that grows across the surface of the ground is called a **stolon**.

There are many other terms referring to the finer details of bamboo and grass physiology but the terms mentioned here should give you a good grounding.

ABOVE Inflorescences come in all shapes and sizes – the panicles of *Pennisetum villosum* just invite you to touch them

ABOVE The fleshy rhizomes of this pot-bound bamboo can be clearly seen. One rhizome has emerged from the soil and given rise to a new culm

NATURE KNOWS BEST

Their absence of flowers in the conventional sense means that grasses and bamboos bring calm and respite, if you need it, from the carnival of colour provided by herbaceous perennials and flowering shrubs. The focus is more on form and foliage and less on hue, although grasses and bamboos do of course bring colour to the garden, albeit from a more limited palette.

Grasses in particular look great in mixed or perennial borders where they can enhance a floral scheme with their subtle shades and arching habits; even the more upright-growing varieties bring welcome movement in the slightest of breezes. Teamed with blooming plants, grasses allow a pause, so the eye can rest a while.

But bamboos are a little different. Grasses easily gel with a bloom-laden planting scheme, thanks to their prairie origins, whereas bamboos can feel somewhat uncomfortable in a floral scheme. They have a quiet, mysterious quality to them that makes them at odds to showy achilleas, alliums and asters and much more at home with modest acers, aconites and arums. Bamboos are stunning near water and make fantastic specimen plants and screens.

The advice I give is to look to nature for guidance. Over the course of this book you will find examples of plants in the wild and of tasteful use in the cultured landscape. Remember, there is a time and a place for every plant; listen to them and they will guide you.

ABOVE RIGHT **Bamboos look more at home in subtle plantings rather than jostling with showy blooms. This *Shibataea kumasaca* really shines out as a solitary planting**

RIGHT **Let nature be your guide. Grasses grow with eye-catching perennials, like these foxgloves, in the wild**

GRASSES

Ornamental grasses are simply exploding in popularity. They are being planted and experimented with like never before, and after many years on the fringes of mainstream gardening, they have finally fallen firmly into vogue. Such are the charms of grasses, I think gardeners will soon be wondering how they managed without them!

In the USA, where gardeners are fanatical about their lawns and where laws exist to prevent homeowners from allowing their grass to grow too long, the worm is turning. Gardeners and professional designers alike are phasing out lawns in favour of more exciting, environmentally friendly options such as plant-filled borders. In fact there are even websites devoted to losing the lawn and reintroducing native grasses and perennials.

A good lawn is expensive and time-consuming to maintain, and many lawn-lovers use fertilizers, pesticides and selective herbicides to keep their green carpet in tip-top condition. On the west coast of America, 60 per cent of all water used goes on watering the grass. But let's be honest – lawns don't actually *do* much, do they? They don't attract wildlife and they also don't bring any transient interest with the changing of the seasons. Do you think it's time that you lost the lawn in favour of more ornamental grass species?

LEFT **A lawn takes a lot of work to keep it in tip-top condition – is it really worth it?**

KEW GRASSBASE

If grasses excite and intrigue you then take a look at Royal Botanic Gardens Kew's GrassBase. It's a detailed database of all known grass species in the world – no mean feat! Don't expect inspiring photographs or design ideas though, because this mammoth document is a research and reference tool.

GrassBase is fully searchable and gives synonyms, descriptions of habit, foliage and flowers, as well as where in the world you might find the grass growing.

If this all sounds a bit too technical and you'd rather just immerse yourself in the sensory delights that grasses have to offer, visit Kew's grass garden. It contains over 550 grass species. There's even a display area showing different types of turf grass. A pristine lawn is championed by some gardeners, whereas others prefer to hack it up in favour of more borders. If this sounds familiar, at least there's something to whet every appetite at the Royal Botanic Gardens!

KARL FOERSTER – A MAN WITH A VISION FOR GRASSES

Karl Foerster was born to gardening parents in Berlin in 1874. He became a garden apprentice before travelling to Italy for further study. Upon his return, Karl began to resurrect his parents' nursery and 'sort the wheat from the chaff' by only growing varieties that were robust and gardenworthy. Although primarily a nurseryman, he also became a prolific horticultural lecturer and writer, as well as undertaking garden design commissions and breeding programmes.

We owe more than 600 favourite garden plants to Karl Foerster, including *Rudbeckia fulgida* var. *sullivantii* 'Goldsturm', *Delphinium* 'Berghimmel', heleniums, salvias and many other perennials and grasses, including *Miscanthus sinensis* cultivars.

In 2001 the Perennial Plant Association selected the wonderful *Calamagrostis* x *acutiflora* 'Karl Foerster' for the Perennial Plant of the Year Award. Karl's daughter, Marianne, continues her father's work to this day.

ABOVE **Karl Foerster loved grasses and he used his nursery to propagate many of the plants we know and love today, such as *Rudbeckia fulgida* var. *sullivantii* 'Goldsturm'**

BAMBOOS

Bamboos are grasses that mean business. In fact it's easy to forget that bamboos and grasses are in the same family, Poaceae. They have such presence and elegance, and were recognized for their gardenworthiness long before other ornamental grasses.

GIANT PANDAS

Pandas are in fact carnivores, despite the fact that almost 100 per cent of their diet is bamboo. They have the digestive system of a carnivore and so can't digest cellulose, which makes up around 50 per cent of bamboo's tissue. Therefore pandas must ingest huge quantities, up to 88lb (40kg), of bamboo every day to keep their digestive systems ticking over adequately. Some research suggests that they prefer certain varieties, but other observations show that these big bears aren't fussy!

ABOVE **Bamboo is the staple diet of giant pandas, despite the fact that they're carnivores**

ABOVE **The thin, whippy growth of this *Pyllostachys aurea* 'Holochrysa' indicates that it is still juvenile. As it matures, the underground rhizomes will swell, giving rise to stouter canes**

GOING UNDERGROUND

Bamboos' rhizomes are their lifeblood. Many bamboos can be razed to the ground but will re-emerge if they have a strong, well-developed rhizome network. A young bamboo will have thin rhizomes, thin culms and relatively few fibrous roots. But a mature, well-established bamboo will have thick, fleshy rhizomes that give rise to thick, strong canes. When a bamboo flowers it usually dies, but if it has plenty of fleshy rhizomes it might just stand a chance of survival. Leptomorph bamboos (runners) have a far better recovery rate than pachymorphs (clumpers).

ABOVE **Bamboo wood isn't wood in the traditional sense. These stunning chusquea culms, and those of all bamboos, owe their solidity to silica and lignin**

ABOVE **In many Asian countries rural villagers are often reliant on the bamboo they find in the forests around them for building materials, utensils and much more**

FOR THE LOVE OF BAMBOO

In countries where bamboo grows wild, this versatile plant is inextricably woven into the inhabitants' lives. Bamboo is an important commodity with significant economic and practical value in most Asian countries and it is also highly symbolic.

In China, Japan, Vietnam and other Asian countries, many everyday sayings and proverbs pertain to bamboo. Because bamboo is a strong, long-lived plant, with a vigorous root system, it represents prosperity, integrity and good luck. It also signifies purity and innocence because of its lack of showy blooms and its clean, simple form.

TOUGH STUFF

As we've established, bamboos are grasses with hard, woody stems. But bamboo wood isn't the true wood of tree trunks. Bamboo culms are impregnated with lignin and silica which cause the stems to harden. High quality paper can be made from bamboo but the paper-making process is made difficult by the presence of silica and lignin. And as a bamboo culm reaches the optimum age for maximum fibre yield, so its silica and lignin concentrations are at their highest levels.

RUN FOR COVER

If you are ever in an area affected by earthquakes, try to stay close to a bamboo grove at all times! Bamboo roots form such a strong, dense mat of fibre that they are said to hold the ground together, even in the event of a severe tremor.

CHAPTER 2

How to grow grasses & bamboos

rasses and bamboos hail from a vast range of natural habitats around the world. Whilst we're unlikely to be able to exactly mimic the conditions of the Himalayas or the prairies of South Africa, we can provide conditions in which grasses and bamboos thrive.

GROWING CONDITIONS

In section 2, the A–Z plant directory, I will give specific requirements for each variety listed. Broadly, however, there are several factors you need to take into consideration before making a purchase – soil conditions, aspect and plant hardiness.

ABOVE On the whole, grasses and bamboos are easy to grow, but, as with any plant, correct positioning is critical to success. This stunning collection of miscanthus, with bamboo as a backdrop, proves that it's well worth spending time choosing the right plants for the right place

To be perfectly honest, grasses and bamboos are not difficult to grow well. Generally, they are not fussy plants and once established in the right position they can almost be left to their own devices. High maintenance they are not! Most varieties should adapt well to a range of conditions, although you may be presented with differing growth habits, leaf colour, proliferation of flowers and vigour, depending on the certain conditions.

SOIL

Take a look at your soil, pick a handful up and feel it; give it a squeeze. Is it wet or dry; sand or clay; heavy, or light and crumbly? You could carry out a pH test on your soil to determine whether it is acidic or alkaline, although most grasses and bamboos are tolerant of either. If your soil is poor and needs improving, refer to the advice in 'Planting' on page 31.

ASPECT

Is your garden in the baking sun all day long, or is overshadowed by tall trees and buildings? Ideally it'll be a mixture of both, allowing you to grow the widest range of bamboos and grasses. Getting the aspect right is really important. A sun-loving grass will sulk in the shade and produce a shadow of the foliage and flowers that it's capable of in bright conditions. And a variety with delicate foliage can easily be scorched when out of the safety of dappled shade.

The aspect also has a bearing on hardiness and as a canny gardener you can use it to your advantage. If you have a bamboo or grass that is tolerant of a range of light levels but isn't particularly cold tolerant, grow it against a sunny wall. At night, when the temperature drops, the wall will radiate the heat it absorbed during the day, giving a crucial few degrees of extra warmth. But aspect doesn't just mean sun or shade; wind is a key factor in whether your plant flourishes or flops.

ABOVE **Some plants, such as acid-loving azaleas, rhododendrons and camellias, are very fussy about their soil, but grasses and bamboos tend to be more easy going**

Winds can be beneficial and refreshing, reducing the incidence of pests and diseases; or ice-cold, scorching vulnerable foliage in the depths of winter; or hot and drying, increasing evaporation and making watering a thankless task. Bamboos tend to be more susceptible than grasses to the burning effects caused by cold winds. In fact many grasses originate from windswept plains and prairies and their fine leaves are a perfect coping mechanism.

ABOVE Use trellis to diffuse the breeze – it's often more effective than solid fencing, which tends to funnel the wind and increase its vigour

ABOVE This *Miscanthus sinensis* 'Adagio' benefits from the residual heat of a brick wall

A gentle breeze usually poses no threat and to be quite honest it's a rare garden indeed that is wind-free. But what may seem like a gentle caress in the balmy days of summer can transform into an icy draught during winter, parching bamboo foliage and lowering temperatures significantly. What I'm saying is, think ahead before you plant and try not to position your specimen in a 'wind tunnel'. If you want to plant in a particularly breezy spot, use wind-tolerant shrubs such as *Griselinia littoralis*, escallonia and elaeagnus, to diffuse the prevailing wind. And consider erecting strong trellises in a similar way, not just around the garden boundaries, but also bisecting it, to lessen the wind's force. Trellises used in this way look very attractive and help to create a sense of mystery as not all areas can be seen at once. Avoid using solid fence panels because they can actually increase the wind's power. Instead, opt for woven types, such as willow or hazel.

ABOVE Whilst you're unlikely to come across tender bamboos for sale in nurseries, you may be faced with grasses that benefit from some protection, such as pennisetum

HARDINESS

There are many bamboos that will not grow successfully in our cool, temperate climate without a great deal of mollycoddling. Some may need protection from cold, whilst a few need shelter from heat. However, it is uncommon to find bamboo for sale in a local nursery that is not hardy in your area, so you can usually buy with peace of mind. Question the staff and try to find out where in the world the variety comes from and what the conditions there are like. Pay particular attention to maximum and minimum temperatures as well as the length of time that these extremes can be tolerated.

You will, however, quite commonly come across tender grasses for sale. The reasons could be that on the whole grasses are simpler, quicker and cheaper to propagate; smaller, so easier to transport; and make a saleable plant more rapidly, so are justifiably planted by some as summer bedding. But if you go out of your way to track down a plant from a specialist grass nursery, chances are you won't want to discard it at the end of the summer. See 'Tender treasures' on page 30 for advice on growing and overwintering non-hardy varieties.

ABOVE *Pennisetum setaceum* 'Rubrum' needs winter protection

TENDER TREASURES

Tender grasses are a real asset in the garden. Many of these grasses have boldly oversized leaves, strikingly coloured foliage, or eye-catching flower- and seedheads.

The easiest way to make tender grasses a summer feature in your garden is to pot them into roomy plastic containers filled with a mixture of loam-based potting compost and slow-release granular fertilizer. Sink the pots in the border after the danger of frost has passed, but be ready with the fleece in case a late one is forecast. As the other border plants grow up around your tender grasses the effect will be seamless. Make sure you water them as you would any other container – they won't have access to soil moisture like the other border plants.

Lift the grasses before the first frosts and allow them to die back in a frost-free greenhouse. Keep them just moist through the winter and if they need repotting, do it in spring before planting out again.

Try this with other tender exotics such as cannas and dahlias – they team fabulously with grasses and other bold foliage plants.

ABOVE **If you love the jungle look, go for bold leaves and mix hardy plants with tender specimens. The hot colours of cannas and tuberous begonias bring the wow factor to this scheme at Compton Acres, Dorset**

PLANTING

There's no mystery to planting grasses and bamboos. As with any other perennial, tree or shrub, preparation of the ground – namely improvement of poor soil – will help a plant get off to a healthy start. It isn't difficult to tell whether you need to improve your soil – just take a look at what's already growing.

If you successfully grow a wide range of plants you can assume your soil is fertile with a good structure. Existing plants that are healthy, strong, well established and, in the main, resistant to pests and diseases, show that you need not worry about soil improvement. Just digging a hole and plonking in your new acquisition will suffice. By all means, fork in some soil improver if it makes you feel better – it certainly won't do any harm.

Bear in mind that you don't want the ground to be too rich because this will promote sappy, floppy growth that may attract aphids. If your soil is healthy but you still feel that you'd like to enrich it, do it thoroughly once, then leave your grasses and bamboos to seek out their own food and fend for themselves. This will make them strong, independent plants that are better able to cope in times of stress, such as drought, extremes of temperature or pest attack.

See also 'Growing conditions' on page 26.

ABOVE **Take a look at what's already growing – if all is well you can be confident that your soil is healthy and that additional plants should flourish without being pampered**

31

ROOM FOR IMPROVEMENT

We all have the occasional disappointment in the garden, the odd plant that just doesn't get off to the flying start you'd hoped it would. But if you survey your plot and a number of specimens are looking peaky – yellowing, lacklustre foliage; susceptibility to pests and diseases; slow establishment; and weak growth – this is a sign that your soil leaves a lot to be desired. This is often the situation in the gardens of newly built properties – see panel opposite.

If this is the case it would be prudent to enrich the soil several months prior to planting by forking in plenty of leafmould, well-rotted garden compost and/or some very well-rotted manure. I say several months because this will give the soil improver a chance to work its magic by enhancing the structure and drainage and boosting the nutrient level. It is always best to dig in soil improvers during late autumn and early winter, then plant the following spring. Harsh winter weather, coupled with all that lovely organic matter, really helps to break up the soil and speed the path to perfect planting.

In fact, if I were in this situation, I'd get a bulk load tipped and fork it into all my borders. Fork another load of soil improver in next autumn and in subsequent years if needed – your plants will soon let you know whether they're satisfied or not.

A TALE OF WOE

I was once called to examine a poorly performing lawn at a new property. The lawn was yellowing, lumpy and looked really shabby. Upon digging down to inspect the soil I discovered that the turf had been laid on just a skimming of topsoil over a bed of rubble. Once the grass had rooted through the meagre layer of soil the roots had become starved and dry as they searched for food and water amongst the chunks of brick and concrete. There was nothing for it but to lift and re-lay the lawn, after digging out all the rubble, of course!

ABOVE **Leafmould makes a wonderful, nutrient-packed soil enricher – it really is worth the 12-month-plus wait while it rots down. Beech leaves make the most fabulous, crumbly leafmould**

SOIL PROBLEMS ASSOCIATED WITH NEW PROPERTIES

- Thin, poor quality topsoil
- Surface compaction due to movement of vehicles, especially those with tracks
- A surface crust often forms and prevents water from soaking down into the soil
- Puddling is another problem associated with surface compaction – its name is self-explanatory!
- Panning is sub-surface compaction, which is due to deep cultivation with earth-moving equipment
- Excess materials, such as building sand, are often buried, creating nutrient-poor pockets. This encourages shallow rooting and starvation
- The builders' perennial favourite – buried rubble. The odd brick here and there will do no harm but expanses of rubble pose all sorts of problems, not least, digging!

Unfortunately, the only way to overcome buried rubble and building materials is to dig them out. Compaction problems can all be remedied with the addition of soil improvers. To alleviate an area of panning under the soil, deep cultivation with a fork will be necessary to break up the hard pan. If left in place, a sub-surface pan can lead to drainage problems.

If you feel that the problem area is too extensive to deal with in this manner, you could consider having a network of herringbone drainage channels installed. They should direct excess water into soakaway pits. A good landscape contractor should be familiar with this technique.

BELOW **Check for builders' rubble; it's often buried under a thin layer of topsoil by unscrupulous contractors**

PLANTING BAMBOO

These step-by-step instructions illustrate the method for planting a bamboo, but they can also be applied to grasses. If you're planting a tenderish, winter wet-hating grass, make sure you position it slightly proud of the soil surface so the crown doesn't hold water and rot during the colder, wetter months.

If you're planting near a lawn like this, you'll need to install a root barrier first – see 'Root barriers' on page 36.

2 Remove the bamboo from its pot. This may be easier said than done. If your specimen is desperate to be repotted or planted its roots may be pushing so firmly against the inside of the pot as to make it irremovable. If this is the case you will have to cut the pot off.

1 Dig a hole a little larger than the plant's pot and fork over the sides and base to loosen the soil and allow roots to penetrate rapidly. If you're adding any soil improver then make the hole twice as big as the pot and mix the organic matter with the removed soil. Water the hole and allow it to drain.

3 It's highly likely that the roots will be circling the pot. This is not a serious problem, as it can be with trees, because new growth will soon spring forth to stabilize the bamboo. However, vigorously circling roots do look rather alarming. Tease the roots and rhizomes out very gently.

4 Lower your bamboo into the hole, making sure that the top of the rootball is level with the soil surface. If the roots were bulging over the top of the pot, sink it down lower so that these are not exposed – you may need to dig out a little more soil. Backfill with the removed soil.

5 Wriggle the soil down the sides of the rootball using your spade to eliminate large air pockets. Firm the plant in well with your heel to stabilize it and prevent wind-rock. Don't be too heavy-footed though; over-compaction will damage the soil structure and starve the roots of oxygen.

6 Water the bamboo in thoroughly. The water needs to penetrate all the way to the base of the rootball and into the surrounding soil. Use your common sense – if there has been a lot of rain recently take care not to overwater – your new bamboo won't thank you for soggy feet.

ROOT BARRIERS

If you'd like to guide a bamboo's roots in the right direction or stop a rampant variety from spreading unchecked, it's essential that you install a root barrier. This may be a purchased, specially made membrane or an improvization using overlapping or mortared slabs. Whatever you choose, it must be sunk down into the ground at least 2ft (60cm) and should protrude above ground by about 4in (10cm). The barrier must also travel the length of the plant's anticipated spread, otherwise the rhizomes will simply sneak around the end.

The use of a root barrier is not ideal; it is far better to plant a variety that will suit your situation, but gardening life is not always that straightforward. Prompt removal of any escaping rhizomes with a sharp knife or spade is essential.

ABOVE **A root barrier should be of strong construction and must protrude above the soil surface. This one is made from recycled rubber**

RIGHT **Accidents will still happen – slice off any escaped culms promptly**

ON THE MOVE

Moving an established plant is never the ideal scenario but in some circumstances it can't be avoided. Relocation can be carried out successfully but timing and preparation are key factors.

If possible, move bamboos and grasses (or indeed any plant) in the autumn. At this time of year the ground should be moist but not frozen or waterlogged and the air cool, but not excessively so. These conditions allow the plant to settle in its new surroundings before the really cold, wet weather arrives. Moving in autumn also gives a plant a considerable period of rest before it has to push into active growth, so stress is kept to a minimum. You can imagine that moving a plant in the height of summer puts considerable strain on a plant's resources, not to mention the time you'll need to spend watering! If an autumn move is unachievable, spring is the next best option. It's also the safest time to move tenderish, winter wet-hating varieties, such as pennisetum.

Lift your bamboo or grass as described on page 53. Set it down on a strong sheet draped

AFTERCARE

Water your plant only whilst it is establishing – through the first two summers – and then afterwards in times of drought. This will encourage it to put on plenty of root growth in a quest for food and water. If you provide everything a plant needs in its immediate root area, what incentive is there to expand its root system in search of soil resources? A wide-spreading root system is to be encouraged because it represents a plant that can fend for itself. It will provide stability, prevent wind-rock and enable the grass or bamboo to cope in times of stress. Providing rich food and an abundance of water may give an appearance of lushness above ground but it will give rise to a poorly developed root system. When you do water, make sure you're very thorough. A quick whizz with the hose on a hot day will probably do more harm than good. If water repeatedly penetrates only the surface of the soil, shallow rooting will be encouraged. Again, this reduces a plant's access to soil reserves and jeopardizes its ability to pull through hard times unscathed.

Feeding in the open ground should be unnecessary. Once your plant is established it will find all it needs in the soil. As discussed earlier in this chapter, if your soil is particularly poor, forking in well-rotted organic matter in late autumn or early winter will provide additional nutrients and enhance the soil structure.

ABOVE **A well-established bamboo in the right spot won't need feeding or watering to keep it healthy and vigorous**

in a wheelbarrow to make heaving it into position at the other end easier. Then replant as described in 'Planting bamboo' on pages 34 and 35. Do make sure the new hole is dug prior to digging up your specimen to minimize time out of the ground. Aftercare should also be followed as detailed above.

RIGHT **Autumn is the best time to move most grasses and bamboos in order to keep stress to a minimum**

ABOVE **The narrow, upright shape of this stipa is complemented by the long Tom pot to make a fun, quirky statement**

CONTAINER CULTURE

Grasses and bamboos lend themselves well to being displayed in pots. If you take into consideration, and are prepared to cater for, their increased dependency on you to provide food, water and space, there's no reason why they shouldn't be as happy and healthy as they would be in the open ground.

When choosing a pot, take great care to make a selection that will complement your plant, providing a balance between foliage and container. The ideal situation is to take your plant with you and try placing it in a few pots until you have a 'eureka!' moment. The right pot can transform a lovely plant into a stunning one.

Pot culture can enable you to grow bamboos and grasses on terraces and balconies or in courtyards and other areas where space is restricted. It also means that you can grow a fairly wide range of varieties in a relatively small space.

MATERIALS

For moisture-retaining properties plastic is hard to beat. Unfortunately, the appearance of most plastic planters leaves a lot to be desired, although more attractive designs are gradually becoming available. Lead is also a great moisture saver but decent-sized containers will be pricey. Lead-look planters made from clay and fibreglass offer an affordable, lightweight alternative. Their manufacture requires only a fraction of the energy used to produce most other types of pot, which makes them an eco-friendly option too.

Terracotta and glazed or unglazed earthenware are the most widely available and popular pots. They are affordable and long-lasting, and come in a never-ending array of colours, sizes and designs. A distinct advantage of terracotta and earthenware over plastic (apart from aesthetics) is their weight. A tall bamboo with a dense clump of canes is a sitting target on a gusty day and a weighty pot will offer significant stability.

Whilst compost dries out faster in porous terracotta and earthenware, I feel that this isn't necessarily a bad thing – frequent, thorough watering gives a healthy turnover of old for new water and keeps the root zone fresh.

SIZE AND SHAPE

The best way to choose a pot is to stand your plant in a range of different shapes and sizes until you find one that looks just right – if you have a keen eye this method usually guarantees a perfect fit. You're looking for a balance between the shape and volume of the top growth and the pot. Whatever you do, don't choose a pot that narrows at the mouth, otherwise you'll have to smash it off when the time comes to repot the plant.

Don't be tempted to choose a pot that's too big because you think it'll last longer. Whilst it isn't the end of the world if you overplant a bamboo or grass, it isn't the best way to get them off to a flying start. The whole effect will be bottom-heavy and out of proportion and varieties that are naturally weaker-growing will often have a sulking period before they put on much growth. By the same token, don't choose a pot that's a snug fit because it's less expensive or will take up less space on your terrace. This is false economy because you'll have to repot your plant before the growing season is out or face a pot-bound specimen that's hungry and difficult to keep moist, due to insufficient compost.

A young bamboo in a 5 litre pot with a diameter of approximately 10in (25cm) should be potted on into a container with a diameter of about 14–16in (35–40cm), then into one about 24in (60cm) diameter, and so on. But as the pot diameter becomes more significant, so will the depth, thus providing plenty of additional root space. When the grass or bamboo becomes too large to repot it should be split (see pages 52 and 53 for instructions) and the divisions repotted or planted out in the open ground.

ABOVE **Metal planters give a contemporary look and retain water well**

ABOVE **Don't choose a pot that narrows at the mouth – you'll have to smash it off unless you just sit your plant inside in a plastic container**

FOOD AND WATER

In the ground bamboos and grasses are perfectly capable of looking after themselves, except perhaps during periods of extreme weather. Even then, if planted in a suitable spot and well established, they should recover from whatever nature throws at them. However, when

ABOVE **The importance of thorough watering is often underestimated**

ABOVE **Just stick your finger in the top of the compost to feel if a plant needs watering**

you choose to confine a plant, you enter into an agreement whereby the plant will continue to bring pleasure and look beautiful as long as you provide all the resources it cannot access due to its imprisonment. For this reason it's always better to plant your specimens in the ground but I won't pretend that I always follow 'horticultural law'. Rules are there to be broken and we gardeners are great ones for experimenting and finding new ways to do things. Gardening is seen by some as a science and others as an art – in reality it's a bit of both.

Watering is an easy task but one that, for some reason, so many people get wrong. Bad waterers fall into two camps. There are the overprotective ones who lavish so much care and attention on their wards that they end up killing them with kindness – overwatering can be as harmful as underwatering. Then there are the lazy ones who are jolted into action only when they see the leaves of their bamboo curling up and turning crispy. You know who you are, so make amends now; incorrect watering over a prolonged period will result in a bamboo or grass that never reaches its full potential.

During the growing season you should water bamboos and grasses when the top 1–1½in (2–3cm) of the compost has dried out. Just stick your finger in and poke around gently – there's no mystery to it! Obviously there are a few varieties that prefer to be constantly moist during the growing season, such as strikingly variegated *Carex phyllocephala* 'Sparkler' and most cyperus species, but these will be pointed out in the plant directory on pages 116–155. When you've established that your plant needs a drink, make sure you soak it thoroughly. Don't just give it a few glugs – use sufficient water to fill the whole pot. As you pour, allow the water to reach the rim of the pot, then pause for a few seconds while it soaks in before continuing. It's no good carrying on pouring while the water is gushing over the rim and onto the ground.

During the winter, containerized plants still need moisture but clearly much less than when they're in active growth and the sun is beating down. If they are out in the open air, rain will do the job for you. But if your pots are on a covered balcony or otherwise sheltered from the rain don't allow them to become bone-dry. A thorough watering perhaps once or twice a month will suffice but of course this depends on the air temperature and amount of sunshine.

As for food, neither bamboos nor grasses are particularly gluttonous. The best option is to mix in granular slow-release fertilizer at the time of planting at the rate specified for the pot size you're using. This information is available on the packaging and can vary a little from brand to brand. Slow-release fertilizer provides nutrients as and when the plant needs them and is influenced by available soil moisture and temperature.

Once the granular fertilizer has been exhausted, apply a general purpose liquid feed once a month from spring to early autumn. Alternatively, you can insert slow-release fertilizer plugs into the compost, but these concentrate nutrients in one area, which is far from ideal.

ABOVE RIGHT *Carex phyllocephala* 'Sparkler' prefers to be kept constantly moist...

RIGHT ...as does cyperus

BEST OF BOTH WORLDS

If you know you'll be taking weekends away through the warmer, drier months, consider planting your bamboos and grasses in plastic containers (for water retention) and sitting them inside terracotta or earthenware pots (for stability and to keep roots cool). If you're away any longer than a couple of days make sure you enlist the help of a reliable plant waterer, otherwise you may return to some rather shrivelled specimens.

ABOVE Terracotta pots are so much more attractive to look at but plastic ones retain moisture – why not combine the two?

POTTING UP

1 If your pot is large and heavy get it in position before planting because it will be difficult afterwards. Stand the plant in the pot and try them in different positions until you're satisfied. Lift the pot onto its feet, making sure that they're evenly spaced around the base to ensure stability.

2 Fill the base of the pot with crocks to aid free drainage. You can either use traditional broken terracotta or chunks of polystyrene. Polystyrene has the added benefit of being able to expand and contract so if the compost freezes and swells it shouldn't crack the pot.

4 Slow-release granular fertilizer should be mixed in with this layer of compost (see 'Food and water' on page 40) and also with the compost you'll use to backfill around the rootball. Don't add more than suggested because it may burn the roots.

5 Position your grass or bamboo in the pot and make sure you've added enough compost in the base to bring the top of the rootball no higher than 2in (5cm) below the rim of the pot. If the roots are exposed on the surface of the rootball, sink it a little deeper.

3 Add a layer of loam-based compost suitable for mature plants. This type of compost takes a long time to break down, unlike peat-based multi-purpose, so is suitable for long-term plantings. It is also weighty so will give stability to the pot and prevent the plant becoming top heavy.

6 Now fill around your plant with more compost–fertilizer mix until it's level with the top of the rootball, firming gently as you go. If the roots are exposed, cover them completely. Spread a layer of gravel, slate chippings or fine bark over the surface and water in thoroughly.

BEST FOOT FORWARD

Always position your containers on pot feet. If you can't get hold of specially made feet or your pots are very large, use bricks instead. Raising pots on feet:

- improves air circulation so roots and pots are less likely to suffer frost damage
- ensures free drainage so roots don't become waterlogged and porous pots don't retain water – especially important in cold weather when a freeze can cause wet compost to expand and burst its pot
- makes life difficult for slugs and snails. Whilst these beasties aren't major pests of bamboos and grasses, snails are rather partial to some fleshier-leaved varieties
- makes earwigs, woodlice and vine weevils feel less at home – they love to hide under pots during the day
- finally, it simply makes the pot even more attractive

ABOVE **Raising pots on feet gives many benefits**

MULCHING MATTERS

It's a good idea to spread a layer of mulch over the compost of potted grasses and bamboos. As well as providing a neat finish, a mulch will help to conserve moisture by slowing down evaporation. It also prevents the compost from blowing or washing away in adverse weather conditions and makes it easy to tug out weed seedlings. The mulch layer needs to be about 1in (2cm) thick in order to do its job properly.

There is a huge range of mulches available to the gardener, from gravel in a range of colours to crushed glass, slate chippings, seashells and even recycled car tyres. Experiment with mulches and find one that really sets off the foliage of your bamboos and grasses, as well as complementing their containers.

ABOVE **A mulch provides a neat finish**

ABOVE **There's a huge variety of decorative mulches to choose from**

MAINTENANCE

Happily, most grasses and bamboos are very low-maintenance plants. This is especially true if they've been planted in well-prepared ground and in favourable conditions. It goes without saying, for example, that if you plant a damp-lover on a dry, sun-baked slope you're going to be forever watering it. Making informed decisions at planting time means you'll spend more time enjoying your plants and less time cosseting them. Refer to 'Situations' on page 62 and also the A–Z plant directory on pages 116–155 for guidance.

All you need to do to ensure grasses and bamboos keep looking their best is some strategic thinning and, for deciduous grasses, an annual cutback.

THINNING BAMBOOS

A clump-forming bamboo will naturally grow into a dense thicket radiating out from the central point. Year on year, new stems emerge around the periphery and in time this urn-shaped fountain of growth can become rather heavy and overbearing. As well as this, varieties with

ABOVE The stems of this *Semiarundinaria yashadake* f. *kimmei* need thinning to show them off to their spectacular best

ABOVE Grasses and bamboos are easy to care for and can be left pretty much to their own devices once established

ABOVE This *Phyllostachys viridiglaucescens* is a perfect example of how stunning a bamboo can be if we are able to appreciate its form to the fullest

particularly decorative stems won't be showing their wares to the fullest if the stems are all rammed up against each other.

The idea is to remove a proportion of the oldest stems to ease congestion and make way for the younger, fresher, usually more brightly coloured growth. In this way you assist the plant in undergoing a cycle of renewal, letting air and light into the centre of the clump. This has the added benefit of keeping the bamboo healthy – free-flowing air will reduce the incidence of pests and diseases and there will be fewer places for nasties to hide.

Fewer stems also mean fewer leaves; this results in a lower rate of transpiration, thus reducing the demand for water, which is very convenient in dry weather! See tip box 'Breathe deeply' (right).

HOW TO THIN BAMBOO

Wear thick gloves and use clean, sharp loppers or a pruning saw to remove stems at ground level. Take care not to damage emerging new growth. Step back and take a look at your progress from time to time to make sure you're creating a balanced effect and not being too lopper-happy! When you're satisfied with the results clean away all the fallen leaves, culm sheaths and other debris that have been trapped

BREATHE DEEPLY

Transpiration is water loss through leaf pores called stoma or stomata. These pores are mostly on the underside of leaves but are also found on the surface. Stomata open and close to allow the exchange of gases – the release of oxygen (a waste product for plants) and the absorption of carbon dioxide needed for photosynthesis (food production). Plants don't mean to release water when their stomata open but it's a necessary trade-off when allowing valuable CO_2 to enter and unwanted O_2 to escape.

Transpiration is reduced when the air is humid because it's laden with moisture; in fact plants can actually absorb water through their leaves in damp conditions. However, transpiration increases in arid, windy conditions as the air effectively sucks water from the leaves.

in the thicket and add them to the compost heap. You can use your prunings as supports around the garden, or why not try weaving them together to create your own garden art?

ABOVE **Use a sharp pruning saw to remove stems at ground level**

ABOVE **Collect debris from between the remaining culms and add it to the compost**

45

TIDYING GRASSES

Deciduous grasses – those whose leaves dry out and lose their colour over the winter – need cutting back on an annual basis. This is best done in two stages. The seedheads borne in late summer and autumn are best left over winter. Not only are they decorative, especially when dusted with frost, they provide valuable snacks for birds during the leaner months. But by midwinter, these seedheads will probably have become very tatty-looking so snip them off along with any broken stems. It's important not to get carried away at this stage though; the dried stems will insulate the crown of the plant from the worst of the winter weather – especially important for more tender species, such as pennisetum. Delay cutting the whole clump to the ground until you can see vigorous new growth appearing, usually late March or early April. For narrow-leaved varieties you should

find that sharp garden scissors are adequate but for toughies, such as miscanthus, use secateurs. The pruned stems can be composted.

ABOVE This is gourmet dining avian style – an assortment of seedheads with a side order of peanuts!

ABOVE Snip out faded blades of wide-leaved evergreens

ABOVE This robin is on the forage for seeds and berries

ABOVE Rake through narrow-leaved evergreens with your fingers

Evergreen grasses can be left to their own devices for the most part. However, if you want yours to look as though they belong on the showbench, a little TLC won't go amiss. For fine-leaved varieties simply rake through the plants during the spring with your fingers to dislodge any dead leaf blades. The blades of some varieties may be razor-sharp so wear gloves if necessary. Wide-leaved varieties are rather a labour of love. You'll have to use sharp, narrow-nosed scissors to cut out dead leaves – nail scissors or needle-nosed garden snips are ideal. Again, compost the debris.

WINTER PROTECTION FOR GRASSES

Most grasses are as tough as old boots but a few are a little more tender, particularly disliking the cold, wet feet that winter can deliver for them.

ABOVE It's safer to overwinter *Papyrus involucratus* in a frost-free greenhouse rather than leaving it in the pond

A covering of crumpled horticultural fleece or dried fern fronds over the crown will keep fussy varieties snug as a bug.

Pennisetum setaceum and *P. villosum* are a couple of popular varieties that benefit from this treatment. Very tender varieties, such as *P. macrostachyum* and *P. x advena* (often sold as *P. setaceum* var. *rubrum*) should be brought into a frost-free greenhouse over the winter. Consider growing them in large plastic tubs for plunging into the border during the summer months.

Most cyperus varieties are tender but as they're most often grown in water a winter fleece covering is rather impractical! Lift the planting basket out of the pool and store just moist in a frost-free greenhouse. Those handy, flexible trugs make ideal winter mini ponds.

WINTER PROTECTION FOR BAMBOO

You'll find few overwintering issues with bamboo, simply because those on sale in any given area tend to be varieties that are hardy in that region. However, wind-burn is a common problem and in severe cases it can completely defoliate a specimen. Think before you plant. If the spot you have in mind suffers beatings from winter winds, then bamboo is not the plant to choose. That said, even a sheltered spot can suffer occasional adverse weather conditions, so keep your eye on the forecast. If high winds are predicted, pin horticultural fleece over the plant – clothes pegs will come in handy!

ABOVE Cover borderline hardy varieties, such as this pennisetum, with a layer of fleece in cold weather

ABOVE Severe wind-burn can have devastating effects, as this chusquea shows

47

PESTS AND DISEASES

Grasses and bamboos enjoy a fairly pest- and disease-free existence. There are a few nasties to keep your eye out for though:

Rust Grasses and bamboos occasionally fall foul of this unsightly fungal infection. It's spread via spores and encouraged by moist, humid conditions. Keep your eye out for bright orange or brown markings on the leaves, and sometimes the stems too. Remove infected growth immediately and any debris from around the plant. Dispose of it in the household waste, not the compost bin. Also try to increase the circulation of fresh air by pruning back neighbouring plants (if practical) or moving potted specimens to a breezier spot. Avoid splashing the foliage with water as far as possible. And if all this doesn't help, spray with a proprietary fungicide, following pack instructions carefully.

Aphids and scale insects These sap-suckers rarely become a severe problem on grasses or bamboos. But a more troublesome problem associated with aphids is sooty mould – see below. Pick off and squash the insects (or scrape off the scales with your fingernail) at the first sign of infestation; caught early you can put a serious dent in a population. If infestations become severe, introduce biological control in the form of parasitic or predatory insects – a perfect excuse to increase the ladybird population! Alternatively, spray with a proprietary insecticide – follow the instructions on the packaging.

Sooty mould This goes hand in hand with an aphid attack. Aphids secrete a substance know as honeydew (just a fancy name for waste

LEFT The orange-brown spots on the leaves of this carex indicate a rust infection

48

black and mouldy as it decays. If an infestation is severe the sooty mould may significantly reduce the amount of light reaching the plant cells, thus inhibiting photosynthesis and therefore hindering food production. Apart from being unsightly, in this way, sooty mould can further weaken a bamboo already under aphid attack. The only way to remove sooty mould is to wipe it away with a soft, damp cloth – a labour of love but worth the effort. Minor infestations on mature specimens won't pose a threat and can be ignored.

Bamboo mite This pest was relatively rare not so long ago but is becoming increasingly prevalent due to lax import and export systems. It is already fairly common in China and North America and is on the increase in the UK. The term 'bamboo mite' is loosely used to refer to any one of 40 or more species of mite that may attack bamboo, including the common red spider mite. More concisely though, the true bamboo mite is *Schizotetranychus celarius*. In a similar way to red spider mite, bamboo mite is found on the underside of leaves and spins fine, protective webs. It sucks the sap from the leaves, creating irregular, paler patches that spoil the look of the plant.

Check your bamboo regularly; if caught early, the best way to deal with the problem is to spray with an insecticide containing bifenthrin. In severe infestations, the only option may be to cut the plant to the ground and burn the crown in a controlled manner. The plant will recover in time.

Of course, prevention is better than cure. Before purchasing any new plant, check it thoroughly for webs and pale blotches on the leaves. Do not purchase any suspect plants and inform the nursery owner so that they can take appropriate control measures.

I must stress again that it's rare for bamboos and grasses to fall foul of pests or diseases. Growing your plants in the right location and keeping them well watered in dry spells is the best way to maintain healthy, happy plants.

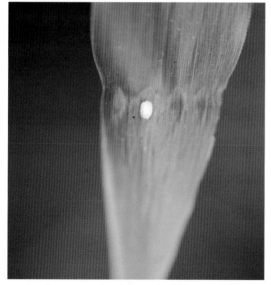

ABOVE **For effective control, scale insects should be treated when the juveniles are active in early summer, before they have 'settled down'. The leaf puckering shown here is a typical symptom**

ABOVE **Sooty mould develops on honeydew secreted by aphids**

PROPAGATION

It's relatively easy to bulk up your bamboo and grass stocks by division or from seed. Cuttings can also be taken from some species but it's rather a drawn-out process and is simply not the logical way to propagate when division and seed-sowing give such reliable results.

DIVISION

This is the easiest and most successful way to increase your bamboo and grass stocks. Both are divided in a similar way and if you've ever split a herbaceous perennial you'll find division of bamboos and grasses comparable.

ABOVE **Most perennials are easily increased by division – grasses are no different**

LEFT **Grasses produce seed in abundance – make the most of it!**

Division of grasses should be carried out in spring when the plants are entering active growth after their winter rest. Split a grass before the winter and the youngsters will sit sulking, possibly even succumbing to the cold and wet. But make your divisions in spring and the new plants will romp into vigorous growth. In fact, many grasses seem to relish being divided; they may put on so much fresh, new growth that by late summer you'll barely tell that the original plant was hacked into pieces earlier in the year.

On the other hand, it's important to divide bamboo well before active growth begins, and while the air is cool and moist, so early spring is the time to wield your pruning saw.

DON'T BE GREEDY

When you decide to split a specimen, be it a grass or a bamboo, you may feel that the clump is sizeable enough to produce a whole family of offspring. Think again. If you make small divisions you'll probably find that the resulting tiddlers grow weakly at best or give up the ghost at worst. And even if they do survive, they'll be slow to establish. It's much more prudent just to divide bamboos in half and grasses into quarters, or in half for less mature clumps.

Large divisions will re-establish rapidly, given the right conditions, meaning that it may be possible to divide again next year or the year after that. Be aware that some slow-growing bamboos will take four or five years before they are up to being split again.

RIGHT These *Molinia caerulea* subsp. *arundinacea* were split earlier in the year yet they still manage to put on a fine autumn show

DIVIDING BAMBOOS

Bamboos have a very tough, rhizomatous root system and attempting to divide a mature, established specimen in the ground is not recommended. If you do want to go ahead and try, be aware that you need to make clean, downwards cuts with a sharp spade. Levering the two pieces apart with back-to-back forks (as is the practice for herbaceous perennials) will damage the rhizomes, not to mention being a near-impossible feat of strength. However, if you have a bamboo growing in a pot, division is a much more reasonable undertaking. You must still take into consideration the tough roots – slicing through them will take a sharp, sturdy saw and plenty of brute strength. Consider enlisting the help of a strapping fellow-gardener if you don't feel particularly muscular!

1 Remove the specimen from its pot – if it's a plastic one you may need to cut it off because the bulging rhizomes could be gripping the inside. Hopefully you haven't been tempted to plant your bamboo in one of those lovely, narrow-necked Ali Baba pots, otherwise a swift blow with a hammer may be the order of the day!

ABOVE **You'll need a strong, sharp saw to cut cleanly through the tough rhizomes**

2 Saw straight down through the crown and roots. Don't use a blunt or flimsy pruning saw because you'll soon become frustrated – use a sturdy, quality tool. If the bamboo is fairly mature or the compost especially gritty the saw will become blunt.

3 Remove any damaged growth and pot up the divisions. Use a weighty, loam-based compost – it won't break down quickly like multi-purpose compost does. Don't over-pot the divisions; use a container that is the same size as the original, or larger if it makes potting up easier.

4 Keep the new plants sufficiently watered and in a cool, humid environment, preferably protected from frost, until they are showing plenty of fresh root growth. A shaded greenhouse is ideal. Cutting down all stems by half will reduce transpiration, putting less strain on your new bamboos' water and energy reserves.

LEFT **Remove the pot from your bamboo when it's due a drink, then give it a good long soak prior to division**

Whilst I'm not advocating that you ever underwater a bamboo, it's a fact that the plant will be easier to remove from its pot when it's on the dry side because the compost and roots won't be swollen. It's a good idea to de-pot the bamboo when it is due for a drink, then soak it in a bucket for an hour or so to plump up the roots before they are divided.

DIVIDING GRASSES

1 Using a fork, work your way around the clump, levering the plant out of the ground as gently as possibly. Start a reasonable distance from the edge of the clump until you ascertain where the rootball begins – you're aiming to keep it intact at this stage. Be patient as you lever and work the plant free a little at a time. The clump will probably pop free all of a sudden as the last roots come loose.

2 Slide the fork underneath and lift the entire grass onto a suitable surface – you may need some help. Get an assistant to help with a sizeable clump by sliding another fork or a spade under the opposite side and lifting with you. If the clump is very heavy, work on a plastic sheet on the ground, but if you can, get the plant onto a potting bench.

3 Varieties with soft, almost non-existent crowns, such as *Stipa tenuissima*, will pull apart easily into smaller clumps – remember though, no more than four! Use a pruning

saw for those with tough crowns, such as *Miscanthus sinensis*. Then there are the types that are toughish but not enough to warrant a saw – most carex varieties fall into this group. Use a couple of hand forks back-to-back to prise the clump into pieces.

4 Replant the divisions straight away to keep stress to a minimum. Pot up into containers that are just a couple of inches wider than the rootball or plant out into a nursery bed until you feel they're large enough to warrant border space. Or plant them straight out into the border (which is what I tend to do). Whatever you decide, keep the new grasses well watered until they're established.

DIVISION IS A PIECE OF CAKE

If the grass you want to divide is planted in the open ground and rather on the large side, digging up the whole clump is difficult. You could use a sharp spade to slice it in half while it's still in the ground and just lift one piece. Or you could remove a triangular wedge (about 45°) from the clump, just like a slice of cake! Why not push the boat out and treat yourself to another slice from the opposite side too? The original clump will soon fill in and replace the missing wedges so by midsummer your tracks will have been covered and no one need be any the wiser.

If you're replanting the wedges out in the border amongst other grasses, shrubs and perennials the initial triangular shape will never be noticed. But if you're going to settle these divisions in pots, simply chop a little off the pointed end to make a chunkier shape. Again, the wedges will soon clump up and any odd shape will be softened in a matter of weeks.

This method works best with larger, looser grasses rather than those that form small, neat mounds. Obviously the missing wedges are much more apparent on the latter.

ABOVE Removing wedges from border grasses, such as this calamagrostis, is a great way to bulk up stocks without disturbing the original planting. In a few weeks the missing bits will be virtually undetectable

ABOVE Try this method with large, loose varieties rather than small, tidy ones, like this neat *Festuca glauca*

WETTER IS BETTER

Water your specimen thoroughly a few hours before you take the saw to it, whether in the ground or a pot. The moisture will help to keep the rootball together as you lift it and reduce post-division stress.

ABOVE **Give plants a good soak a few hours before lifting**

ABOVE Grasses produce plenty of seed every year. This *Miscanthus nepalensis* seedhead has become light and fluffy – the sign that its seeds are ripe

SEED

Once a grass is established, whether in a pot or the ground, you'll be treated to a plentiful supply of seed every year. Bamboos are an entirely different story. They can take 100 years or more to bloom, and once they do, they often rapidly decline in vigour and eventually die. This knowledge, coupled with the fact that bamboo flowers are less than spectacular, is a reason not to wish for a floral display any time soon. However, if you do have a very mature bamboo that starts to bloom, all is not lost. The seed produced should germinate with a high success rate.

BLOOMING BAMBOO

When a bamboo flowers, something rather spectacular happens on a global scale. Amazingly, all plants of the same clone of a species flower at the same time, regardless of where in the world they're growing! They could be wild or cultivated, enjoying midsummer or enduring winter, in England or America, aged 70 years old or 170; somehow, something triggers them off and no one is quite sure what.

This global phenomenon has been the subject of much research, with scientists putting forward a range of suggestions as to the possible triggers. But no one is sure, and the short, infrequent windows of opportunity that flowering bamboos provide make research work difficult, to say the least. To make matters even more bizarre, there are two different types of flowering – partial flowering and complete flowering.

In partial flowering, blooms appear on only part of the plant – often just one stem. But pollination is most successful when there is an abundance of blooms, so partial flowering usually amounts to a wasted opportunity. Looking on the bright side, because flowers are only carried on a small part of the plant, stress is minimal and they usually suffer only a slight setback.

Complete flowering usually puts strain on bamboos' resources to the extent that they don't recover, or, if you're lucky, take several years to start back into healthy growth. Every stem is laden with panicles of blooms, with leaves sacrificed to make way for them. The production of new canes grinds to a halt and existing juvenile ones are put under strain as they too bear flowers. Food production slows dramatically with

LEFT **In the event of flowering, running bamboos, like this sasa, may survive...**

disastrous effects; the energy expended in flower initiation quickly depletes that stored in the rhizomes. This usually spells the end for clump-forming (pachymorph) bamboos because their rhizomes are short and less abundant, with every one being heavily depended on for food by the canes arising from it. But it's often a happier story for running (leptomorph) bamboos – their longer rhizomes are more plentiful and, though severely knocked back, often have enough food reserves to aid the eventual recovery of the plants.

If you do encounter the mixed blessing of a flowering bamboo in your garden, don't dig up and discard the root system after the plant blooms. Wait for three or four years – it may be building up energy reserves in order to spring back into growth.

ABOVE **...but clumpers, such as this *Thamnocalamus crassinodus*, are unlikely to live**

GROWING FROM SEED

Grasses and bamboos are easy to grow from seed. There is usually a high germination success rate, but bear in mind that whilst some species will appear in just a few days, others may take a few months.

Seed should be gathered and sown as soon as it's ripe, not before! This is very important – the seed will not be viable if you harvest the inflorescences too early. Wait until the flowerheads have opened fully and the seed is clearly visible. This should be approximately three months after the inflorescences first appeared, give or take a little. Some species will give you a clear sign when their seed is ready, such as miscanthus, whose inflorescences change from firm, silky plumes to dry, fluffy tassels. After a couple of years of growing and observing grasses, you'll know when it's time to act.

The problem is, when the seed is just right for you to sow, it's perfect for your feathered friends to eat too. But to be quite honest, if you're on the ball there will be plenty for you and the garden birds too. Keep a look out – when there's higher than usual avian activity, rush out with a paper bag, shake some seed in, and then leave the rest as valuable snacks.

If you would rather have the first bite of the cherry, when you think the seed is almost ripe, erect a tent over your plant using fleece or net and some canes. Alternatively, snip a few stems and store them somewhere cool and dry to finish ripening. Lay a cloth under the stems to catch any falling seeds.

ABOVE **Look for the fluff! The seed in this miscanthus seedhead is ripe...**

ABOVE **Some seed falls of its own accord as soon as it's ripe**

ABOVE **When ripe the seed coat will split open to reveal the (often tiny) seed inside. Use tweezers to separate the seed from its coat and the fluffy hairs that help it to float on the breeze. If left in place the coat may rot and take the seed with it before germination can occur**

ABOVE **...but this one has a few weeks to go yet**

59

SOWING SEED

1 If the variety you're growing has seed that falls of its own accord when it's ripe, lay a sheet on the ground for a couple of days to catch some, unless you've taken stems indoors of course. For varieties that hold onto their seed, pick it off between finger and thumb and drop into an envelope.

2 Fill a seed tray or several 3½in (9cm) pots with seed compost and tap down sharply to settle the compost. The surface of the compost should be no less than ½in (1cm) below the rim of the pot or tray to allow space for watering. Peat or coir-fibre pots or modules may also be used – see 'Biodegradable pots', below.

3 Water the pots thoroughly and allow them to drain, then place the seed on the surface of the damp compost. Use tweezers to position the seed if it is very tiny, spacing it evenly and allowing four seeds per pot. If you're sowing in trays, allow about 2in (5cm) between each seed and its neighbour.

BIODEGRADABLE POTS

Peat or coir pots are very useful if you're planning on propagating a large number of seedlings, perhaps to create sizeable drifts in the border. They can be planted straight out in the ground where they will quickly rot down without inhibiting root development. Or if you want to pot the seedlings on as usual into larger containers, biodegradable pots enable you to do so without root disturbance.

RIGHT **Make sure you soak the pots thoroughly before sowing – they absorb moisture like a sponge**

5 Place your sowings in a coldframe, a cool greenhouse or a sheltered spot outdoors. Keep your eye on the pots – the compost needs to stay just moist but never wet. The seed may germinate in about a week or may need longer, depending on the species. Overwinter the seedlings under cover, then prick out in spring – see 'Pricking out' (below).

4 Cover the seed with a thin layer of vermiculite. I prefer to use vermiculite rather than compost because it's lightweight and also allows light to be bounced onto the seed to encourage germination. You can use a thin layer of sieved compost if you prefer. Label the pots and water in gently.

ABOVE **Soak pots of compost thoroughly before sowing. If over-zealous watering is carried out after sowing, the seed will be washed to the edges of the pots**

ABOVE **Make sure you label your sowings – grass seedlings have a tendency to all look very similar!**

PRICKING OUT

In spring prick out the seedlings into individual 3½in (9cm) pots. Use a loam-based potting compost that has an appropriate structure and nutrient content for young plants. At this juvenile stage of growth a fertilizer-rich formulation could do more harm than good.

Ease the seedlings out of their pot and use a dibber or an old fork (the culinary type!) to ease the young plants apart. Pot each individually and grow on until the plants have bulked up and you can just about see roots protruding from the base of the pot. The young grasses or bamboos can then be potted on again into larger containers – this time in a loam-based compost suitable for mature foliage plants. Don't delay repotting because it can cause a considerable check in growth due to starvation and lack of water.

ABOVE **Ease the roots apart gently to avoid damaging them**

CHAPTER 3

Situations

Wherever you garden there is a grass or bamboo for you, and probably a great deal more than one! Grasses and bamboos grow in such a range of different situations around the world that even if you consider your plot to be a particularly difficult one, these wonderful plants will enable you to weave a tapestry of colour and texture. Even dry shade, that bane of gardeners' lives, can be lightened, brightened and reborn with a few swathes of *Luzula sylvatica* and *Millium effusum* 'Aureum' teamed with lily turf, *Liriope muscari* and *Geranium phaeum*.

In addition to being attractive plants, grasses and bamboos are very useful, providing groundcover and screening, height, bulk and much interest in ordinary and extraordinary situations. When buying bamboo, always talk to a knowledgeable member of nursery staff about varieties that will grow successfully in your conditions.

ABOVE **In tricky dry shade team** *Luzula sylvatica*, **the greater wood rush, with...**

ABOVE **...lily turf,** *Liriope muscari...*

EXPOSED AND COASTAL AREAS

If you live by the sea, on the fens or plains, in hilly regions or any other wind-beaten location, you'll know that not just any old plant will stand up to Mother Nature. Seaside plants have to put up with salt-laden air but many grasses, thanks to their narrow leaves, just take it in their stride – take the marram grass that colonizes European, African and American coastlines (see 'Beside the seaside' on pages 64–65).

Bamboos aren't always the best choice for very windy or seaside locations because harsh gusts can leave them looking burnt and beaten. Many bamboos originate from still, humid, sheltered conditions and so their leaves may be soft, delicate and easily scorched. But if your garden is lashed by salty air, don't despair, there is a clutch of toughies that will stand up to coastal conditions. These include the fairly widely available *Phyllostachys aureosulcata* (yellow groove bamboo) and the very variable *Chusquea culeou* which relishes well-drained soil – perfect for sandy, coastal sites.

ABOVE **It's so exposed but a wide range of grasses still manage to thrive despite baking sun and lashings from wind, rain and snow**

ABOVE ***Chusquea culeou*** **tolerates well-drained soil so can be grown on a range of difficult sites**

ABOVE *...Millium effusum* 'Aureum'...

ABOVE **...and *Geranium phaeum*, seen here growing under silver birch trees, interwoven with ammi**

IS IT TOUGH ENOUGH?

If you're unsure whether a grass will thrive in an exposed area, examine its leaves before you buy. Do they feel tough, waxy or leathery, particularly on the underside? Can you see fine hairs and/or ridges on the upper leaf surface? If the answer is yes, then this grass will probably thrive because it has mechanisms in place to cope with windy, drying conditions.

DRY AREAS

As I've already described in 'Exposed and coastal areas' (see page 63), grasses have highly developed coping mechanisms for dealing with dry air. But what about dry soil? What can you plant to fill that bed under the trees, the one that doesn't get much sun and has soil like dust? Or what about that bank that bakes hard and becomes virtually impenetrable to water during the summer months?

Instead of just accepting that the soil is dreadful, enrich it annually with organic matter as outlined in 'Planting' on page 31. This will help retain moisture and improve the soil structure.

Soil improvement will go a long way to increasing the range and health of the specimens you plant but you will still have to work with what you've got to a great extent.

ABOVE **The blue colour and smooth, waxy cuticle indicate that this fescue will stand up to wind, sun and dry or salty air**

BESIDE THE SEASIDE

Marram grass is a perfect example of a xerophyte – a plant that grows in a harsh environment such as a desert or coastline and has adapted its structure to reduce evaporation and transpiration. There are two species: *Ammophila arenaria* is native to European and north-west African coastlines; and *A. breviligulata* colonizes the eastern coast of North America. Ammophila withstands harsh conditions as far north as Iceland because of its acutely honed physiological makeup. Whilst marram grass is considered invasive in some areas, such as California where it has been actively introduced, there is no doubt that it does the invaluable job of stabilizing dunes and lessening coastal erosion. And it can do this because of its incredible root system that reaches deep underground to tap into hidden water reserves.

However, you can also take a long, hard look at whether other factors can be changed to improve matters. For example, is your dry shade caused by a demanding, unsightly conifer hedge that does nothing to improve the aesthetics of your plot? Despite being a big job, would removal of the hedge be the best option for opening up your gardening possibilities in the long term? Just think – you could even replace it with a bamboo hedge! (See 'Privacy and hedging' on page 74.)

Not quite as difficult to plant as dry shade, but still a challenge, is dry sun. Soil that is dry to begin with is often of poor structure and low nutrient content. Add to this a baking from the sun and the stress on most plants is considerable. But many grasses can cope admirably in just such conditions. Think about

ABOVE *Stipa calamagrostis* will tolerate poor, well-drained soil and still put on a fantastic show

Marram grass's long, narrow blades are covered with a waxy coating called a cuticle; its function is to prevent water loss and protect from salt. To further minimize transpiration, the leaf blades roll tightly in dry weather to shield the stomata from the drying wind and keep them in as humid an environment as possible. Sharp hairs and ridges trap moisture and additionally the stomata are sunk in pits.

So with all those defence mechanisms above ground, what's happening below? Ammophila roots are unbelievably tough. Their rhizomes spread rapidly and are encouraged by fresh layers of blown sand. As the marram grass stabilizes more sand and the dunes grow larger, the leaf blades lengthen so they are still able to protrude from the sand. And as the leaf blades grow, so more roots are sent forth. Marram grass is a pioneer plant; it is usually the first plant to colonize an area of sand. Organic matter

ABOVE Marram grass is a pioneer plant – it will grow where others don't dare!

and nutrient levels subsequently increase, thanks to the presence of pioneer plants, and other plants can then begin to grow.

ABOVE **Many sasa species will continue to thrive in dry shade.**
Sasa tsuboiana **is particularly reliable**

the plants you see growing on patches of waste ground, railway embankments and scrubland – grasses always make an appearance, don't they? But I'm not necessarily suggesting you allow the varieties you spot in these locations to colonize your garden; there are many cultivated varieties that are blessed with more attractive attributes and will grow in similar conditions. In addition to being more pleasing on the eye, cultivated varieties, such as *Stipa calamagrostis*, are generally less invasive so they won't cause borders to take on a wasteground appearance!

Bamboos are less tolerant of dry, sunny conditions. In the wild many relish heat and will grow in direct sun as long as it is accompanied by high humidity. Others will tolerate drier soil if they are afforded cooler temperatures and some degree of shade. The most successful bamboos in dry shade are sasa species, many of which make excellent ground cover. Their leaves are usually quite large and during the winter they develop a characteristic bleached edge that is really very attractive and brings interest to a dark, dingy corner.

THE KING OF BAMBOOS

The largest bamboo species in the world is *Dendrocalamus giganteus*. It commonly grows up to 98ft (30m) in height and its culms reach over 1ft (30cm) in diameter. The leaves are anything up to 18in (45cm) long and 2½in (6cm) wide.

In 2003, staff at the Bamboo Institute of Yunnan Normal University discovered a specimen of *D. giganteus* that towered to an unimaginable 151ft (46m) tall and had canes 14in (36cm) wide. It was found growing in Menghai county in south-west China and was part of a cultivated bamboo forest. Just try to visualize a plant 46m tall!

It's the equivalent of a building 12 storeys high. The incredibly broad canes of *D. giganteus* are sawn up and used as buckets and stools, among other things, or are kept in long lengths to use as scaffolding or hollowed out to make piping and water channels.

This species, sometimes called 'the king of bamboos', thrives in a moist, sunny spot but will tolerate drier ground in shade. Don't get your hopes up for including one in your patch of dry shade though – because unfortunately (or perhaps fortunately!) it isn't hardy below 41°F (5°C) so it can't be grown below zone 11. Still, you can dream...

DAMP AREAS

Bamboos and grasses have a natural affinity with water. There are oodles of exciting grasses that can be planted in or beside water, from those that don't mind an occasional dose of wet feet, to those that relish life in the bog garden, or even the pond margins. And a handful of bamboos will tolerate very damp ground, though they prefer not to be waterlogged, and certainly not during the winter months.

Many gardeners develop an instinct, a kind of sixth sense that helps them to place plants. They detect that if a plant looks at home, like it really belongs, then it usually does. If you fancy honing this technique, start with damp-loving plants – they're easy to spot.

Bamboos, grasses and indeed any plants that thrive in dampness are usually the ones with bolder, more luxuriant foliage, exhibiting little of the tough leatheriness of xerophytic species (see 'Beside the seaside' on pages 64–65). Bowles' golden sedge, *Carex elata* 'Aurea', is simply stunning arching over a pond, its acid-yellow leaves turning golden as the season progresses. And when it produces its contrasting dark brown flowers on tall, flexing stems it resembles a kind of graceful firework. But those vivid leaves are soft and easily bent and spoiled by strong winds – this is no grass for a cliff-top garden!

A truly stunning waterside garden can be created with clever plant associations. Think about using bold foliage, such as *Gunnera manicata*, *Ligularia dentata* 'Desdemona' or 'Britt Marie Crawford', and *Rheum palmatum*, to contrast with the narrow leaves of your grasses and the slender, arching bamboo stems. Think too about the reflections you'll create – whatever you plant will have double impact next to a pool – what a bonus!

If you have the garden space and your pool covers a decent area, consider giving bamboo a somewhat free rein and allow a sizeable grove to form along one bank of your pool.

ABOVE *Carex elata* 'Aurea' is a wonderful waterside grass and will even tolerate having its roots lightly submerged

ABOVE The overall form and foliage of *Chimonobambusa tumidissinoda* is graceful and distinctive

ABOVE The curious stems with their swollen nodes are pretty eye-catching too!

ABOVE This phyllostachys isn't actually growing in the water, its feet are firmly on the bank. But the deeply arching stems and wonderful reflection give the feeling that this beast is a real water baby!

In this way, bamboo creates a wonderful transition between water and garden, as well as offering stunning reflections. The widely available *Pseudosasa japonica* and *Chimono-bambusa tumidissinoda*, with its strange but wonderful swollen nodes, are ideal for creating this effect and will flourish in damp conditions. But bear in mind that just because an area of ground is next to a pond, it isn't necessarily damp – if your soil is more free-draining your options are open to plant any bamboo that takes your fancy, as long as it's hardy.

PROTECT YOUR POND

Take care when planting bamboo next to a pond with a butyl or other liner of thin construction. Bamboo roots are notoriously strong and purposeful and they will easily puncture this type of pond liner. If your pond is of this construction it's essential that you install a reliable root barrier along the full length of the area. Use a purpose-made product or a row of paving slabs laid vertically in a trench and overlapped or mortared at the joints. Make sure the top of the barrier is higher than the top of the pond liner and promptly sever any rhizomes that snake their way over the top.

Concrete-lined ponds, by their very nature, aren't flexible and if there is any subsidence, weak points and hairline cracks can occur. Bamboos are opportunists and the persistent rhizomes of more thuggish varieties will take advantage of any chance to breach a barrier that stands in the way of them and expansion. If your water level appears to be mysteriously dropping check the lining, which may need patching or replacing.

Perhaps you are planning to install a new pond and want to use a flexible liner. Liners are now available that have an exceptionally high tensile strength and are very resistant to tearing and root penetration. Good aquatic shops should be able to help you and there are also some online suppliers. Don't rely solely on these liners though – advanced as they may be – you should use a root barrier as well.

ABOVE *Gunnera manicata* makes a real statement as a waterside planting. *Cyperus longus* in the foreground is a little past its best but is still packing in the autumn colour

CONTAINERS

To my mind, grasses and bamboos in containers are a joy. Growing an individual plant in a pot allows its whole form and habit to be admired. And whilst grasses and bamboos enjoy interaction in a border situation where they can flop over, grow through and support each other, when potted, plants' shapes can be fully appreciated from top to bottom, side to side and without distractions. Of course, this effect can be achieved in the garden by specimen planting, but this style should be used sparingly. Take pampas grass, cortaderia, for example; this genus is only just beginning to regain some vestiges of dignity after being plonked in the middle of lawns on an all-too-frequent basis.

FUTURE NEEDS

It is important to consider the future needs of a plant if you want it to grow successfully in a pot. Let's stay with pampas grass; you know that it's going to get very big, so you should be prepared to pot it on regularly (probably yearly) and eventually be able to accommodate, not to mention afford to purchase, a very large container. If this isn't possible, then another option may be to plant it out in the garden when it outgrows its space on the terrace.

ABOVE This *Eragrostis curvula* 'Totnes Burgundy' is perfect in a long Tom pot. The tall, narrow container allows the delicate foliage to droop gracefully in a way that would be unachievable in the ground

ABOVE Yearly repotting will be necessary to accommodate pampas grass; because of its eventual size, pampas should be viewed as a fairly short-term container plant

The growing of bamboos and grasses in pots also stretches the boundaries of what varieties you can grow. Borderline or downright tender varieties can be moved in and out of doors as the weather changes.

Play around with ideas – containerizing plants is not limiting; in fact it allows you to have vegetation where it would not otherwise grow. If you have a set of wide steps, place a potted bamboo or grass at each side of every other tread; stick to the same variety for maximum impact. Cluster several potted grasses and bamboos together to create a living montage. Choose varieties that enjoy the same growing conditions but have different growth habits and make sure the containers complement each other. Stick to odd numbers in a group for a more pleasing, 'designery' feel.

ABOVE **Regular, thorough watering is essential if containerized plants are to remain in top condition**

TOP POT TIPS
Don't underestimate the amount of care you must give your containerized plants.

- Don't allow the soil in pots to dry out. Even during the winter soil should be kept moist.
- If very cold weather threatens, wrap pots in bubble wrap and secure it firmly in place to prevent the pot from freezing solid. All pots should also be on feet, if you've taken my earlier advice.
- Thinning bamboo canes and raising the leaf canopy somewhat not only exposes the fabulous bare canes, but it will also reduce the leaf area and thus reduce transpiration levels. In turn, the demand for water will be lower, but don't think it gives you a free rein to put your feet up!

See also 'Container culture' on page 38.

ABOVE **Group pots of different shapes and sizes together**

NEW WAYS WITH GRASSES

Many grasses have a delightfully arching habit and when planted in the open ground they tend to drape themselves all over their neighbours, the lawn edge (where they end up getting clipped) and the soil. To show these varieties off to their full potential why not plant them in a roomy hanging basket or a tall, relatively narrow pot, where their graceful, usually very fine foliage can fall unhindered? Evergreen *Carex buchananii*, with its burnt orange-brown, hair-like leaves and dark brown, bobbly flowers on lax stems, is perfect. So too is *Eragrostis curvula* 'Totnes Burgundy'; again, the foliage is hair-like, this time bright green, strongly tinged deep red, and the dramatically drooping flower stems create a cascading effect. Or try sweet-as-sugar *Agrostis nebulosa*, commonly known as cloud grass. It doesn't have a weeping habit but the airy, candyfloss effect is lovely up close in a pot or a low hanging basket. *A. nebulosa* is an annual and very easy to grow from seed.

MOVING ON OUT

If you're trying your luck with tender grasses and bamboos in pots, think ahead and make your containers mobile in case a sudden frost threatens. Ready-made pot stands on wheels are available from most garden centres or if you're a DIY enthusiast try making your own from a wooden frame mounted on castors – you'll find these at the hardware store.

This isn't just handy for tender varieties, it's also perfect for moving plants around to alter your display when you just fancy a change of scenery!

ABOVE **A wheeled pot stand will make life easier. Ready-made ones are readily available or try making your own**

ABOVE **Cloud grass, *Agrostis nebulosa*, is great in a pot where you can gently run your fingers through its seedheads**

CHOOSING GRASSES

If you only have a small space in which to garden, container culture is your best friend. Choose wisely at the outset and the plants you buy will be growing successfully in pots for years to come.

Chances are you'll want year-round interest so choose evergreens or grasses that hold their form through the winter. *Carex conica* 'Snowline', *C. morrowii* 'Ice Dance' and *C. oshimensis* 'Evergold' make great specimens with their brightly variegated foliage and fluffy brown flowerheads. Use *Festuca glauca* or *F. amethystina* to create a lovely contrast with ice-blue, needle-like foliage, topped off during early summer with fans of sparkler-like flowers that hold their shape and bleach to sand colour as they age. For height choose a dwarf miscanthus. Whilst it won't stay green, it'll desiccate to cornfield gold and later palest blonde, all the while retaining its fluffy plumes held on rigid stems. Try *Miscanthus sinensis* 'Dixieland', a variegated variety that will grow to around 5ft (1.5m) in sun or dappled shade. Or if that's a little tall for you, how about *M. sinensis* 'Gold Bar' with its vivid gold zebra stripes – it will reach about 2ft 6in (75cm).

ABOVE **Plant *Festuca amethystina* in a pot and enjoy its needle-fine, richly coloured foliage all year round**

BELOW ***Carex morrowii* 'Ice Dance' is bold and bright enough to light up the darkest winter day. It forms a robust, well-behaved clump too**

PRIVACY AND HEDGING

Have you got a boundary fence that just doesn't reach high enough to offer a feeling of real privacy? Most fences between neighbouring gardens reach 6ft (1.8m) and any person above average height knows this just isn't enough to provide seclusion when you want to don your swimsuit and take a dip in the hot tub!

Bamboo is second to none for creating a living screen and there are many suitable varieties. Conifers, a long-time favourite in the hedging department, don't offer the versatility and contemporary feel that bamboo does.

Like any of its hedging rivals, bamboo can be clipped to keep its shape. And any culms that emerge out of line can be severed to maintain neatness – installation of a root barrier is the best way to keep this task to a minimum. Better still, choose a well-behaved variety, such as *Phyllostachys aureosulcata* f. *aureocaulis*, whose bright yellow culms are stunning against an ivy-clothed wall or fence. Try *Hedera helix* 'Atropurpurea' for its dark green leaves that become purple as the weather turns colder.

If you're after a screen that is total, dense and virtually impenetrable opt for fargesia. Their canes are slender, their leaves small and narrow and their manners impeccable. They form a tight clump and never outgrow their welcome by sending out runners. However, because of their refined demeanour you'll need to plant them close together. *Fargesia nitida* has an eventual clump width of just 3ft 3in (1m) at the base, although its canes do fan out gracefully towards their tips. *F. nitida*'s height of 10ft (3m) is perfect for creating privacy without the overbearing feeling that a Leyland cypress hedge (x *Cupressocyparis leylandii*) can inflict.

LEFT **What more could you ask for in a hedge?** *Semiarundinaria fastuosa* **has been given an Award of Garden Merit by the Royal Horticultural Society for its charms. It even grows naturally in a straight(ish) line!**

It isn't just bamboo that can offer privacy; some grasses are a force to be reckoned with. Take *Arundo donax*, the giant reed, for example – its stems can reach a lofty 20ft (6m) in temperate conditions or more than 33ft (10m) in warmer climes. This is a dramatic, back-of-the-border perennial, producing robust, shimmering flower plumes. The strikingly variegated variety *A. donax* var. *versicolor* is widely available and there are several other less common, but equally attractive, variegated ones. Variegated varieties will tend to be less vigorous than their plain-leaved counterparts.

ABOVE **If you don't believe a grass can be a hedge, think again! This** *Arundo donax*, **overshadowed (but only just) by a eucalyptus, proves that it's up to the job of providing privacy**

ABOVE **The thick, striking culms of** *Phyllostachys atrovaginata* **create a hedge with a difference**

If you want an extra exotic look seek out *A. donax* 'Macrophylla' – its leaves are even wider than the species.

A boundary need not be a formal hedge comprised of the same plant. If your borders are deep, mix bamboos and tall grasses along the back, coming lower as you reach the front. *Miscanthus* x *giganteus* is another great grass for a border backdrop. It resembles *M. sinensis* but on a larger scale. It's more vigorous and reaches 10ft (3m) or more, maturing quickly into an impressive clump. Despite its stature, you can plant *M.* x *giganteus* without fear because it is a sterile hybrid, so can't seed about. This variety puts on growth so rapidly that it is being trialled for use as a biofuel crop. Soon we may be relying on miscanthus power to take us where we need to go and to heat our homes!

LEFT Towering at the rear of this border, *Miscanthus* x *giganteus* is everything you expect from a miscanthus – on a huge scale

BAMBOO HEDGE TIPS
Follow these simple guidelines to achieve a successful screen:
- Don't plant too close to a neighbour's fence or neglect to install a root barrier unless you know they are keen to share. Culms making an unwanted appearance on the other side of a boundary have signalled the sticky end of many a neighbourly friendship.
- Do choose your bamboo with care. If you have set your heart on a variety that has a

LEFT *Hibanobambusa tranquillans* makes a beautiful hedge with its large leaves and spreading habit. This fine plant is also tolerant of dry soil but it will spread more rapidly in search of water. Install a root barrier to guide it in the right direction

RAISING THE CANOPY

Once your bamboo hedge has settled in you can beautify it further and create a dramatic look by raising its canopy to expose bare canes. Simply take a pair of sharp garden scissors or secateurs and snip off the leaf stalks up to the desired height. Make sure you clip the petioles close to the main culm to avoid any unsightly 'stubble'. Stand back regularly and survey your handiwork – it's easy to get carried away.

You could just tidy up the bottom 2–3ft (60–90cm) or so, or create something more striking by removing the leaves to about halfway up the culms. Don't be tempted to go much above halfway though – plants need leaves to feed themselves! Either take the canopy on every cane to the same height to create an arresting, contemporary feel or stagger them to give a more natural, grove-like look.

RIGHT **These stems of** *Phyllostachys vivax* f. *aureocaulis* **were just begging to be revealed**

tendency to run, take very seriously the advice to install root barriers all around the designated eventual perimeter of the hedge.
- Don't plant closer than 3ft 3in (1m) apart because the bamboos will compete for water and nutrients fiercely, providing you with a really rather sickly looking screen. Fargesias can be planted a little closer if an impenetrable hedge is desired.
- If you plan to trim your bamboo hedge, in cooler areas, do it once early in the season and be thorough. Subsequent growth will cover your cuts and give a lush effect. However, if you're in a warm spot, little and often is more acceptable because new growth will shoot rapidly. It is preferable, and

extremely therapeutic, to use topiary shears – the single-handed ones forged in one piece are best.
- If you've had a hard day at the office go out in the garden, do some trimming and feel the Zen-like tranquillity spread through your mind and body! But only you know whether you have the patience and time to trim your hedge with hand shears; of course, it may not be practical on a long run. In this case use a hedge-trimmer with care to avoid ripping at the stems.
- Promptly remove any stems that pop up outside the allotted line of the hedge to maintain a neat appearance, rather than that of an uncontrollable thicket.

CHAPTER 4

Planting styles

Whilst the notion of creating a 'theme garden' initially fills me with dread, if done with taste and restraint, it can be very successful. Designing a scheme that conjures up images of far away lands or favourite places can be a delight. And gardening is a very personal, subjective pastime – what appeals to one gardener may be the antithesis of what appeals to another. So whether reconstituted stone Fo dogs, lanterns and Buddhas are essential in your Oriental garden, or whether it will be more a case of carefully raked gravel and a few thoughtfully placed rocks, plants are the painting on your canvas. As such they can make or break the effect you want to create. Whether we're talking about bamboos, grasses or any other plant, there are no hard and fast rules when making selections, but if you look to nature you will be guided well. For example, if the leaves are grey or bluish, with a waxy or downy coating, the plant will suit a seaside garden. If the leaves are dark, with a purple underside, this indicates that the plant will thrive despite low light levels. Perhaps the foliage is particularly fleshy – a Mediterranean style or dry, gravel garden will be the right setting for this succulent specimen.

ABOVE Plant associations can catapult a scheme from mediocrity to magnificence. The clever teaming of black, silver and purple creates a look that is arresting but subtle. It achieves modernity without resorting to the use of gimmicks

ABOVE This show garden uses blocks of planting, including *Stipa tenuissima, Centaurea montana, Geranium phaeum* and *G. phaeum* 'Album', *Stipa gigantea*, aquilegia, digitalis, salvia and iris beneath silver birch to prove that a modern scheme can be successful without sacrificing the plants

Grasses and bamboos can go a long way to setting a scene, from the backdrop, whether bold and commanding or designed to fade into the further landscape, to the 'wow' plants, the stars of the show that take pride of place at the very front of the border and in carefully positioned pots. But the success of grasses and bamboos in your landscape, whether it amounts to rolling acres or a suburban 'postage stamp', also depends on clever plant associations. Contrasting and complementary colours and textures are a pure delight to experiment with. The narrow, pale green and white foliage of *Miscanthus sinensis* 'Morning Light' is gorgeous alone but place it in a bed with dark, smooth-leaved *Cotinus coggygria* 'Royal Purple', vivid lilac, wiry-stemmed *Verbena bonariensis* and dusty looking *Salvia officinalis* 'Purpurascens' and it will positively glow. Add a generous smattering of *Allium sphaerocephalon* for their egg-shaped, burgundy flowerheads in early summer and you've got a scheme to turn heads and make jaws drop in envy. Such is the power of plants.

ABOVE **Grasses play an important part in this show garden, which was designed by the author for the National Amateur Gardening Show. Lucinda also built and planted the garden, along with a team of skilled landscape gardeners. The garden won Best in Show and a Large Gold Medal; it showed that a modest front garden can accommodate vehicles without having to pave over the whole lot. The garden was constructed on a slope to highlight an effective way to deal with the increasing problem of surface water run-off**

COASTAL AND GRAVEL GARDENS

I would say without reservation that bamboos do not lend themselves to the creation of a seaside-look garden, regardless of whether your plot is anywhere near the coast. If you want to grow bamboos by water, save them for a traditional or Japanese-style water garden, not a gravel garden. Remember what I said in Chapter 5 'Damp areas' (page 67) about gardeners developing a feel for what's right and what's not? Now is the time to exercise this sixth sense. Whilst some varieties of bamboo will continue to

ABOVE **Blue is the colour!** *Elymus magellanicus* **is a fabulous coastal grass, thanks to its waxy, blue-grey foliage**

produce lush foliage in coastal conditions, if grown in a seaside location they should be in a garden evocative of their native settings, not in a stereotypical seaside garden with driftwood, low-growing succulents, beach pebbles and such like. Bamboos can work wonderfully near the sea, just not in a coastal-style design. But rules are made to be broken and this is just my design ethic – you may decide differently and prove me wrong.

Look for grasses with glaucous and blue- or grey-green foliage. The most well-known of these is probably *Festuca glauca* 'Elijah Blue' but try also *Elymus magellanicus*, a glowing, almost metallic blue-green. *Helictotrichon sempervirens*, or blue oat grass, forms a neat, evergreen mound and bears fans of blonde flowerheads on flexible stems.

As well as the blue crew, there are many more grasses evocative of the seaside, such as *Stipa gigantea*, the fabulous giant golden oat grass, also known as giant feather grass. Its neat mound of narrow, evergreen foliage is nothing to get excited about but when it flowers, well it's absolutely breathtaking. Strong, slender stems, up to 8ft (2.5m) in height, carry wonderful open panicles of golden flowers that flutter on the breeze and catch the light to give a glittery effect. And these flowerstems last for months, giving a feeling of depth to any coast-themed border. Their height doesn't limit the placement of this versatile plant because the whole effect is one of gauzy transparency. Plant it in drifts if you have the space but a single plant is enough to draw admiration and create movement.

Love them or loathe them (and if it's the latter you need to give them another chance) pampas grasses and seaside gardens feel so right together. Granted, most specimens you're likely to see will be the ubiquitous *Cortaderia selloana* and, while they make magnificent plants, they do get pretty huge – up 10ft (3m) in height and 5ft (1.5m) in spread. If your plot isn't particularly

ABOVE Golden oats, *Stipa gigantea*, introduces a fantastic sense of movement. The stems of this sturdy evergreen will sway in strong coastal breezes without breaking

ABOVE This pampas grass remains in pristine condtion, despite its position in a cliff-top garden

large, this grass will be the dominant feature, so try a more diminutive species. *C. fulvida* is the smallest one you'll find, reaching 5ft (1.5m) in flower with a spread of 3ft 3in (1m). Its plumes droop gracefully and they're altogether more delicate than their more robust family members.

This species is often confused with *C. richardii*, another delightful plant, but another biggy. And to make matters worse, they seem to share the same common name of 'toe toe', so if size matters to you, be absolutely certain which plant you've got in your trolley before you buy.

81

COASTAL CRAFTING

There are plenty of design tricks you can use to make visitors – and you for that matter – feel as if they've just stumbled through the sand dunes and into your coastal retreat, even if you're miles from the beach.

Bank up the ground in places to produce gentle undulations – when spread with gravel they will give the suggestion of dunes. Allow an informal pathway to snake its way between these mounds. If space allows, include forks in the path; one may lead to a secluded seating area and another to an interesting feature of some kind, maybe a driftwood sculpture or an urn gently bubbling over with water. If your garden receives plenty of sun (and if it doesn't I would suggest that you rethink the idea of a seaside garden) make sure you plan for seating areas that make the most of the light. The main outdoor dining area should be located close to the house for convenient access to the kitchen. If possible, position this important area so that it's bathed in the warming rays of the evening sun. A second, more informal set of table and chairs could be positioned to catch morning and/or afternoon light.

Punctuate planting with found objects, lobster pots, driftwood and coils of rope. Don't underestimate the power of the vertical – a few attractive timbers of substantial proportions (such as railway sleepers) positioned securely in an upright fashion will act as exclamation marks and bring excitement to your scheme.

ABOVE **Allow grasses to self-seed amongst the gravel. Here,** *Carex praegracilis* **catches the evening light**

ABOVE Grasses, including calamagrostis, paint a picture of light and admirably stand up to the elements in this coastal garden. A golden gravel mulch provides a link to the beach below

Pebbles play an intrinsic part in beach life. A small grade can be used as a mulch around plants; a larger grade used to create the illusion of a dry river bed meandering its way to meet the sea. Heaps of large pebbles or boulders can be used as simple sculptural elements.

MAKING SEASIDE SPIRES

Tall stacks of pebbles are really effective – you'll need to drill them using a masonry or diamond-tipped bit, then pile them up on metal rods. The steel rods used to reinforce concrete are inexpensive and can be easily sourced from builders' merchants.

Make stacks of different heights and snake them through the border or position together in groups of three.

The pebbles on each stack can be all about the same size or can be graduated, smallest at the top, to give a spire effect. These stacks look great amongst planting that echos their shape – try the foxtail lily, *Eremurus robustus*, *E. stenophyllus* or any other species of this glorious, fleshy rooted perennial. It thrives in sandy, well-drained soil and looks stunning weaving amongst that other striking spire-bearer – pampas grass, of course.

ABOVE Combine drifts of lofty eremurus, foxtail lilies, with pebble stacks for a sculptural effect

COAST-STYLE PLANTING

It isn't out of the question to plant a coastal garden solely with grasses. There is such a wide range of suitable varieties that contrasts in texture, colour and form can easily be achieved. But if you would like to ring the changes, you could also include phormiums, cordylines, yuccas and agaves in the scheme to provide bolder forms without deviating from the basic leaf shape that sets the style.

For the planting of a coast-style garden use an overall palette of muted colours, such as grey, silver, blonde and soft purple, with the occasional splash of acid-yellow, hot pink, bright mauve, sky-blue or flame-orange. Think plants such as *Euphorbia myrsinites*, *Armeria maritima*, *Verbena bonariensis*, *Erigeron glaucus*, *Linum narbonense*, *Eschscholzia californica*, *Limonium latifolium* and eryngium (sea holly). Lavender, sage, thyme and rosemary are all aromatic, shrubby herbs that can cope with the rigours of coastal living, whether real or imaginary. Given a baking on a sunny day they will emit their uplifting, fragrant oils and carry you to the cliffs of a Greek island, overlooking the white sand and clear, azure sea.

Regardless of whether you stick just with grasses or mix in perennials and shrubs as well, plant in drifts and don't be afraid to leave bare ground – it will become a feature in its own right when covered with gravel and will allow space for self-seeding if you take a laid-back approach. Some of the most effective coast gardens are mulched all over with gravel in a soft shade of sandy gold, meaning that areas without plants simply feel as though they have been reclaimed by the beach. If you feel the mulch looks a little overbearing at first, don't worry. Given a season the plants will settle in and spread to soften the scene no end. See also 'Exposed and coastal areas' on page 63.

ABOVE **The long-lasting flowerheads and white-bloomed stems and leaves of** *Echinops bannaticus* **'Taplow Blue' make an enduring statement in the coastal garden**

ABOVE **Pennisetum, teamed here with rosemary,** *Rosmarinus officinalis*, **catches the afternoon light**

ABOVE *Crithmum maritinum*, or rock samphire, will seed its way onto gravelly ground and into crevices

ABOVE The fleshy purple-pink leaves and jewel-like flowers of *Sedum telephium* 'Matrona' will withstand the rigours of coastal life. Poorish soil is best to prevent sappy, floppy stems

ABOVE *Achillea*, yarrow, is an unfussy perennial – just give it lots of sunshine and well-drained (but not bone-dry) soil. This clear, pale yellow cultivar is *Achillea* 'Goldstar'

ABOVE Agapanthus is a fabulous seaside plant with its attractive strappy foliage and sturdy drumsticks of blue, white or lilac blooms

ABOVE The finely divided foliage and cheeky button flowers of santolina will stand up to wind and salty air

JAPANESE GARDENS

Bamboo and Japanese gardens go hand in hand. China has the most diverse selection of native species, but Thailand, Japan, Burma, Vietnam, Korea and other East Asian countries also have rich collections. It must be noted that bamboo grows in the wild far beyond East Asia, to Australia, South America, India and Africa, but it is the Japanese style that typifies traditional use of bamboo in the domestic and public garden. Japan is famed for its classical gardens that often centre around a tea house, said to represent a simple forest cottage. These beautiful gardens provide havens of peace and tranquillity and are an intrinsic part of the ritualistic Japanese tea ceremony. In fact, many of the utensils used in the tea ceremony are crafted from bamboo.

Many Western gardeners seek to recreate the Japanese style and indeed there are plenty of garden societies that offer guidance on the art. At first the design appears simple because of the lack of fuss and floral distraction. But the positioning of every rock, every plant and every curve in the path has a symbolic meaning and requires careful consideration. The creation of a Japanese garden is an exercise in restraint.

ABOVE AND OPPOSITE **This wonderful tea house is the focus of the Japanese garden at Compton Acres in Dorset. Work commenced on the garden in 1924 and it is reputed to have been designed and built by Japanese architects and craftsmen. The Japanese garden at Compton Acres is widely regarded as one of the finest in England**

CLOUD TOPIARY

Form is of utmost importance when choosing and maintaining plants for a Japanese garden. Pruning, topiarizing and miniaturization are key skills. Shrubs are often trained to represent ancient trees and a garden is designed to suggest a wider landscape.

Cloud topiary is a beautiful, very sculptural way to train shrubs. It involves removing some branches and stripping foliage and sideshoots to about halfway along remaining ones to leave them exposed. The foliage left at the branch tips is then clipped into rounded forms, reminiscent of clouds. This form of topiary is evocative of the manipulated, idealized shapes created in bonsai, but in a way that simply involves clipping, rather than miniaturization through crown and root pruning and binding.

Cloud topiary is traditionally carried out on yew, *Taxus baccata*; box, *Buxus sempervirens*; and various pinus species. If you don't fancy trying your own hand at cloud topiary, pre-trimmed specimens can be purchased from garden centres – but at a price.

ABOVE **Whilst this carefully clipped shrub is part of a public display in Hong Kong Park, its manicured form is typical of those found in Japanese gardens**

PLANTS FOR THE JAPANESE GARDEN

Use plants thoughtfully and sparingly. A Japanese garden should be calming, with raked gravel and carefully placed rocks used to suggest rivers, islands and mountains.

When choosing bamboos stick to those with a naturally neat habit that can easily be groomed and kept within bounds. Low-growing varieties, such as *Pleioblastus argenteostriatus* 'Akebono' or 'Okinade', are excellent; the former reaches just 20in x 30in (50cm x 75cm) and the latter a little larger. *Pleioblastus pygmaeus* is a vigorous, spreading variety, but it can be clipped regularly to form gently undulating mounds. *Fargesia* species are graceful, dense, upright and well behaved and vary in height from 6ft 6in (2m) to over 16ft 6in (5m).

Grasses can be used to suggest flowing water as they blow in the breeze or to punctuate a scene. *Hakonechloa macra* 'Aureola' and other varieties have wonderful drooping leaves, complemented by unshowy, sparkler-like flower panicles in late summer. Variegated varieties show the most intense colour in light shade but all tolerate full sun. In autumn the leaves become suffused with deep red from the tips upwards.

Carex oshimensis 'Evergold' is a striking, evergreen grass with clear, bright foliage. It forms a tidy clump and its narrow leaves arch in a well-behaved manner. They're complemented in early summer by short, stiff stems topped with fluffy, brown bottlebrush flowers.

If you'd like to choose a real showstopper, but one that works its magic in a thoroughly tasteful manner, plant sweeps of *Imperata cylindrica* 'Rubra' (also known as 'Red Baron' or blood grass). Its leaves stand perfectly upright, without seeming stiff, and a gentle breeze will send a contagious ripple through the blades. This grass will tolerate dappled shade but really must be positioned in the sun to appreciate its beauty to the fullest. With the light behind it, every leaf glows an unbelievably vivid red.

OTHER PLANTS TO INCLUDE

- Ferns, look out for *Athyrium niponicum* var. *pictum*, the Japanese painted fern
- Topiary – *Buxus sempervirens*, *Taxus baccata*, pines
- Mosses to form cushions and to grow on rocks
- *Acer palmatum*
- *A. capillipes*
- *A. griseum*
- *A. shirasawanum* 'Aureum'
- *A. japonicum* 'Aconitifolium'
- *Acorus gramineus*
- Deciduous and evergreen rhododendrons and azaleas, especially dwarf varieties
- *Nyssa sinensis*
- *Pinus mugo*, *P. mugo* 'Mops'
- *P. pumila*, *P. pumila* 'Compacta'
- *P. parviflora* 'Adcock's Dwarf'
- *Pittosporum tobira*
- Prunus, ornamental cherry – many varieties to choose from
- *Reineckea carnea*

This is not an exhaustive plant list, merely a starting point. The art of Japanese gardening is a large and complex topic and time should be spent studying the many publications on the subject if an authentic garden is to be created. Of course, it may be that rather than follow the rules to the letter, you simply wish to capture the mood of Japanese gardens. If this is the case, use your artistic licence as you see fit and be prepared to excuse yourself to any Japanese visitors you may have!

RIGHT **This wonderful plant association shows** *Hakonechloa macra* **'Aureola' flowing into** *Ophiopogon planiscapus* **'Nigrescens' (black grass), giving the effect of rushing water. Black grass isn't actually a grass at all, it's a narrow-leaved perennial**

ABOVE *Imperata cylindrica* 'Rubra' gives carpets of glowing colour with its strongly red-suffused leaf blades. Plant in swathes for the most stunning effect

ABOVE The Japanese maple, *Acer palmatum*, brings grace and vibrant colour to a Japanese garden. There are many beautiful varieties with a range of habits from weeping to strongly upright. *Acer palmatum* 'Bloodgood', pictured here, has a lovely upright, branching habit and provides exceptional autumn colour

VISIT A JAPANESE GARDEN

The best way to get a feel for the true spirit of the Japanese garden is to see one first hand. Here are a few of the best around the world:

- Compton Acres, Dorset, UK
- Tatton Park, Cheshire, UK
- Golden Gate Park, San Francisco, USA
- Portland Japanese Garden, Oregon, USA
- Hakone Gardens, Saratoga, California, USA
- Brisbane Botanic Gardens, Toowong, Queensland, Australia
- Himeji Gardens, Adelaide, South Australia
- Ogrod Japonski, Wroclaw, Poland
- Buenos Aires Japanese Garden, Argentina

If you wish to visit gardens in Japan, Kyoto boasts many beautiful ones open to the public. There are, however, public gardens of note all over Japan – garden design is considered to be one of the highest artforms.

BELOW **The Japanese part of the gardens at Apple Court in Hampshire, UK, is small but delightful.** *Hakonechloa macra* **'Aureola' bows down to the pool like a shaggy mane, showing autumnal bleaching, red flushes and drooping, sparkler-like flowerheads. Pines, ferns, clipped** *Buxus sempervirens* **and acers all set the mood admirably, and a carpet of** *Soleirolia soleirolii* **(mind your own business) completes the scene. The fiery maple on the right is** *A. palmatum* **'Sango-kaku'**

The oldest Japanese garden in the USA is the Japanese Tea Garden in San Francisco's Golden Gate Park, first conceived in 1894. It was largely designed and developed by Baron Makoto Hagiwara, a well-regarded Japanese landscape designer, who imported plants, statues and more from Japan.

Very sadly, when the Second World War broke out, Baron Hagiwara and his family were imprisoned in concentration camps and his beautiful garden fell into disrepair. When the war was over the slow process began of restoring the garden to its former glory. Thanks to generous donations and much hard work, the Japanese Tea Garden is now one of the most highly regarded tea gardens outside Japan. Baron Hagiwara's great, great grandson, Erik S. Hagiwara-Nagata, continues the family tradition of excellence in horticulture to this day.

If you would like to recreate an authentic Japanese tea garden of your own, you can select from this list of bamboos planted in the Golden Gate Park. The list has been kindly provided for this book by Mr Hagiwara-Nagata himself. The names in brackets are the Japanese common names.

- *Bambusa multiplex* 'Alphonso-Karrii' (ho-o-cjiku)
- *Chimonobambusa marmorea* (kan chiku)
- *Chimonobambusa quadrangularis* (shikaku dake)
- *Fargesia murielae* (xian zhu)
- *Fargesia nitida* (jian zhu)
- *Phyllostachys aurea* (hotei chiku)
- *Phyllostachys nigra* (kuro chiku)
- *P. nigra* 'Henon' (ha chiku)
- *Pleioblastus simonii* (me take)
- *P. humilis* (hirouzasa)
- *P. pygmaeus* (ne-zasa)
- *P. viridistriatus* (kamuro zasa)
- *Pseudosasa japonica* (ya dake)
- *Sasa palmata* (shakotan chiku/chimaki zasa)
- *Semiarundinaria fastuosa* (narihira dake)

ABOVE *Sasa palmata* has big, bold foliage and holds its leaves in a palm-like arrangement, hence the botanical name. It's rather a thug so do install a reliable root barrier

ABOVE Black bamboo, *Phyllostachys nigra*, forms a well-behaved clump of tall, slender, graceful stems

WATER GARDENS

Bodies of water, no matter how large or small, give a garden another dimension. Where lawns and hard surfaces stop light in its tracks, water reflects it, amplifies it and draws it down into its very heart.

Water shimmers with the colours and shapes of objects around it – the sky, structures and, of course, the plants. A gracefully weeping bamboo is a truly breathtaking sight as the morning light bounces its reflection onto the surface of a pool. And a carefully chosen sweep of grass bordering a pond helps to marry the water with the landscape around it.

Grasses at the water's edge also provide a fantasic hiding and mating place for frogs, toads, newts, dragonflies. In fact all manner of

RIGHT The stems of these two papyrus species, coupled with lush iris foliage, make a strong vertical contrast with the bulbous boulder and the flat plane of the water in this pool in Hong Kong Park

ABOVE This vibrant show garden at BBC Gardeners' World Live relies almost entirely on grasses and bamboos to bring height and movement to an otherwise fairly flat, static scheme

ABOVE This delicate-leaved bamboo is growing wild on the banks of the river in Erawan National Park, Thailand. Along with ferns, it relishes the dampness and the shade provided by overhead trees

friendly wildlife will be attracted by a pond and its surrounding vegetation, so if you like the idea of gardening in tune with nature, a pond is essential. And, if you needed any more encouragement, frogs and toads eat slugs, and dragonflies eat midges and mosquitos – very good reasons for attracting these beneficial beasties onto your plot.

WHY DO GRASSES AND BAMBOOS WORK SO WELL WITH WATER?

The vertical lines of grasses contrast to stunning effect with the strong horizontal plane of a body of water. Bamboos are often a captivating combination of the two – their stems being the verticals and their leaves held gracefully on or near the horizontal.

ABOVE **Beneficial creatures, such as dragonflies...**

ABOVE **...and frogs, are attracted to water gardens**

ABOVE **This handsome bamboo brings so many positive elements to this scene. It is strongly vertical but also dramatically weeping, and its powerful form is reflected to give double impact**

MINI PONDS

A body of water doesn't have to be large to have garden-enhancing properties. If you garden in a small space why not create a mini pond in a large container? Simply plug the drainage holes with silicone and paint the inside with bitumastic emulsion to form a watertight seal. Position rocks under the water at different heights and perch grasses and plants on them in hessian-lined mesh baskets.

ABOVE **It may be fairly low on colour, but this watery show garden at Chelsea Flower Show is certainly big on form and texture**

WHAT DO ROOFS AND ORNAMENTAL GRASSES HAVE IN COMMON?

Thatchers use reeds or straw to work their magic. Their reed of choice is *Phragmites australis*, a rampant grass that can reach up to 10ft (3m) in height and can spread indefinitely. Despite being commonly known as Norfolk reed, much of this durable material is now imported from Eastern Europe and Turkey. This is because many of the original East Anglian reed beds have been lost and the remaining ones are unable to keep up with demand. Turkey, Hungary and other Eastern European countries have little demand for *P. australis* but do have extensive natural reed beds.

If you are fortunate enough to have a large pool or lake in your garden, *P. australis* makes a fine waterside planting. Otherwise consider planting some in a large container in which the soil is kept constantly moist.

P. australis 'Variegatus' is a very attractive and less invasive variety, reaching just 6ft 6in (2m) in height. It has bold, golden yellow-striped foliage and boasts flower panicles that are a striking combination of bright yellow and deep purple.

NITROGEN IS GOOD – BUT NOT IN A POND!

Make sure you use aquatic compost when planting in the pond. It is much more dense and weighty than ordinary compost so it won't float away. More importantly, it doesn't contain any fertilizers or chemicals that are harmful to aquatic life.

Nitrogen fertilizers cause algae blooms that block valuable light, use up essential oxygen supplies and choke plants and aquatic animals. As the smothered plants decay they produce more nitrogen, so encouraging further algae growth. This phenomenon is known as a 'bloom' because it happens rapidly, producing billowing clouds of algae.

ABOVE *Phragmites australis* is a force to be reckoned with. It looks very dramatic when naturalized along the banks of a large pool

ABOVE Where the Lymington River flows into the Solent, across from the Isle of Wight, *Phragmites australis* grows wild on the marshes

OPTICAL ILLUSIONS

It's important to bear in mind that if your pool is self-contained (with a watertight lining), the ground around it may actually be very dry! If this is the case you'll need to create the illusion of lushness because achillea, lavender, artemisia, festuca and other dry-loving plants will look very out of place in a water garden.

The luxuriant foliage of bamboo will suggest damp conditions and, unless you happen to have a friend who's a bamboo boffin, no one will be any the wiser that the varieties you've chosen favour drier soil. Try *Yushania maculata*, *Thamnocalamus tessellatus* or *Drepanostachyum microphyllum*. A mixture of different heights, habits and leaf shapes will create as interesting a scene as possible.

As for grasses, any yellow- or golden-leaved varieties look great next to water and will provide contrast to the deep green bamboos. *Luzula sylvatica* 'Aurea', with its bright acid-yellow foliage and brownish yellow flower panicles, is hard to beat. Its sibling, *L. sylvatica* 'Marginata', is lush-growing and its leaves have an attractive creamy trim. Plant it where you can get close and appreciate its subtle charms.

The stipas, and especially the old favourite *Stipa gigantea*, are stunning in drier ground near water. Be sure to place them where their seedheads can be mirrored for double wow factor. And if you don't feel you have space for *S. gigantea*, try *S. gigantea* 'Pixie' – a relatively new selection from Apple Court in Hampshire. It grows to just 4ft (1.2m) but has the same wonderful habit, so is perfectly suited to the smaller plot.

Ferns also have strong associations with water. Try planting *Asplenium scolopendrium* (hart's tongue fern); *Dryopteris filix-mas* (male fern); *Polistichum setiferum* (soft shield fern); *Polypodium vulgare* (common polypody); and *Adiantum pedatum* (maidenhair fern).

ABOVE **Plant *Luzula sylvatica* 'Marginata' to give a lush carpet of glossy, evergreen foliage. This hardworking, subtly variegated grass will tolerate dry shade**

GRASSES FOR THE POND

In the water
> Cyperus species
> *Eriophorum angustifolium*
> *E. latifolium*
> *Glyceria maxima* 'Variegata'
> *Schoenoplectrus lacustris* subsp.
>   *tabernaemontani* 'Zebrinus'

At the water's edge or in the bog garden
> *Arundo donax* 'Versicolor'
> *Carex elata* 'Aurea'
> *C. pendula*
> *Cyperus involucratus*
> *Juncus decipiens* 'Curly Wurly'
> *J. effusus*
> *Phalaris arundinacea* var. *picta* 'Picta'
> *Spartina pectinata* 'Aureomarginata'

You will find that many of these grasses will be tolerant of varying depths of water. Experiment with them – there are no hard and fast rules. See 'Damp areas' on page 67.

ABOVE Ice cool, *Phalaris arundinacea* var. *picta* 'Picta' creates a dramatic waterside statement

ABOVE *Carex elata* 'Aurea' is stunning on the moist banks of this jungly pond. It really lightens and brightens the scene and contrasts with the surrounding lush greenery

ABOVE **If you have the space, plant bullrushes (typha species) with...**

ABOVE **...native *Iris pseudacorus* for a naturalistic effect**

ABOVE **In autumn *Cyperus longus* begins to collapse gracefully into this pool after a summer of providing stunning architectural foliage and flowerheads**

PRAIRIE STYLE

Prairie planting, also known as 'new European style', has caught on in a big way over the past few years. And it's hardly surprising! This informal way of planting creates a garden that's a haven for wildlife and gives the feeling of an ever-changing, texture-rich, living painting.

Prairie style aims to summon to mind the North American grasslands, rich with a diversity of native perennials and grasses. In fact prairies are affectionately known as 'seas of grasses'.

The steppe-like landscape of a bona fide prairie is too dry to support a forest, but not dry enough to become desert. It receives just the right level of rainfall to support grasses and perennials. Bamboos do not feature in prairie planting schemes in any way.

FROM PRAIRIE TO BORDER

Prairie planting offers virtually year-round interest, from the first shoots pushing through the ground in spring, to the swelling, billowing swathes of high summer, through the burnished shades of autumn and, finally, the frosted seedheads of winter. Cut a prairie planting to the ground in late winter or early spring and the cycle can begin again.

The term prairie planting may strike fear in your heart – it sounds wild, unruly, meadow-like. Well in a way it is, but trust me, it's a good way. Prairie planting takes all the best bits of wildflower meadows, refines them, beefs them up a bit and spits them out in glowing ribbons of colour to create the most hazily stunning herbaceous borders you're ever likely to experience.

ABOVE **This border at Knoll Gardens, Dorset, gives a strong nod to the North American prairies, with its large, loose drifts of grasses, eupatorium (left),** *Echinacea purpurea* **'Leuchtstern' (right) and** *Rudbeckia laciniata* **'Herbstonne' (rear)**

No one type of bold leaf or attention-grabbing bloom steals the limelight; it's more a case of creating a soft, muzzy mingling of textures and shades, something like looking at a Jackson Pollock painting through squinted eyes.

Prairie borders aren't dominated by any single species, rather a tapestry painted by a 50:50 mix of grasses and perennials.

PRAIRIE PERFECTION

Before you become too excited you must realize that authentic prairie planting will only enjoy true success in full (or near-full) sun. If your light levels are approaching anything more than lightly dappled shade, forget it. Prairies also depend on fertile, free-draining soil. This is in contrast to traditional English meadow-style planting where we are advised to impoverish the soil as far as possible to give poor-soil tolerant wildflowers a fighting chance against vigorous native grasses. The grasses used in prairie planting are not thugs, nor will the robust perennials allow themselves to be overpowered.

ABOVE **Silky, pale golden flowers of *Stipa calamagrostis* catch the light amongst wiry stems of *Verbena bonariensis***

ABOVE **Remember that a true prairie is bathed in sunshine — yours should be too. Here *Miscanthus sinensis* 'Krater', backed by sanguisorba, tolerates early morning shade in anticipation of the rising sun**

99

PRAIRIE PLANTS

Aim for a roughly even mix of grasses and perennials.

Grasses

Choose medium to tall grasses with fabulous seedheads such as:
Bouteloua
Calamagrostis
Chasmanthium latifolium
Chionochloa conspicua
Elymus canadensis
Eragrostis
Hystrix patula
Miscanthus
Panicum
Pennisetum
Sporobolus heterolepis
Stipa

Perennials

Achillea millefolium, A. filipendulina
Amsonia tabernaemontana
Asphodeline
Asphodelus
Aster novi-angeliae
Astrantia
Baptisia
Echinacea purpurea
Echinops
Eryngium
Filipendula
Foeniculum vulgare 'Purpureum'
Helenium
Liatris spicata
Lythrum
Monarda
Morinia
Perovskia
Physostegia
Phlomis
Rudbeckia
Salvia
Sanguisorba
Sedum
Solidago
x *Solidaster luteus*
Stachys coccinea, S. macrantha, S. officinalis
Thalictrum
Verbena bonariensis
Verbascum
Veronica
Veronicastrum

ABOVE Plant grasses and perennials with a bold hand for high impact

ABOVE Showstopper *Echinacea* 'Sunset' could steal the limelight in a prairie border. Team it with feathery grasses to give a hazy veil

You may wish to supplement this plant list with seed-raised varieties. Remember to go for gutsy flowers in preference to the more delicate British natives. And don't worry – American natives are just as attractive to bees, butterflies and other beneficial insects and birds.

ABOVE Fennel, *Foeniculum vulgare*, gives a see-through effect, similar to that of *Verbena bonariensis* but rather more low-key. Bronze or green will do the job

ABOVE The oat-coloured inflorescences of *Calamagrostis* x *acutiflora* 'Karl Foerster' echo the strongly upright form of neighbouring purple lythrum

ABOVE Weave a ribbon of stately *Verbascum olympicum* through your prairie – it'll certainly be a talking point

ABOVE Hot pink spires of *Veronica spicata* 'Fotfuchs' (red fox) are as stunning in bud as they are in bloom

101

PLANTING A PRAIRIE BORDER

No doubt you've read or heard some of the 'rules' of garden design and the dos and don'ts of creating a planting scheme. It's common practice when laying down a herbaceous border to plant in groups of three or five. Well you can forget that! Aim for for broad swathes of planting woven together in a seamless quilt of colour and tactile extravagance. To achieve this effect, plant in groups of nine at least, but preferably 11 or more.

Obviously the size of your plot will dictate the dimensions of your own personal prairie but you can still achieve boldness in a relatively small border. Go for fewer different plant varieties but keep the ribbons of colour and texture large-scale. The importance of depth should never be underestimated if you really want to capture the essence of a prairie. Don't set aside a long, narrow strip; it's much better to make the border deeper and sacrifice some length. Or consider digging out an ellipse-shaped border to be viewed from all sides.

Height is so important in the prairie style. If you choose the right plants and paint them into the soil with a bold hand you'll be waist-deep or more, out in the grasslands with the wind in your hair, the sun on your face and the sound of swaying grasses in your ears.

ABOVE **Forget planting in threes! This swathe of lythrum feels like it stretches as far as the eye can see**

PRAIRIE ON A SHOESTRING

If you can't afford the large number of plants needed for a full-on prairie scheme, consider spacing out and planting about half the number you need. This will still give a decent show but it won't be as full or intense. Make sure you halve just the numbers, not the range of varieties, and plant over the full area. At the end of the first season collect and sow seed of grasses and perennials and divide or take cuttings from others in spring. Plant the youngsters out as soon as they're ready – having lived with the border through the previous season you'll know where the gaps are. Take photographs and make notes in the first year to remind yourself of any areas that need a bit of extra colour or height.

ABOVE **The prairie border can be bulked up in subsequent years by propagation of existing plants. Perennial and grass species, such as this *Pennisetum villosum*, will come true from seed but varieties and cultivars should be propagated by division**

COTTAGE GARDENS

The drifts of soft, blousy colour synonymous with traditional English cottage gardens have a lot to answer for. They have lured generations of gardeners into the web of addiction that is plantaholism. Yes, gardeners have their switch flicked by an immeasureable range of influences, but the romance of cottage gardens has captured the imagination of more than a fair share. A well-designed garden has the ability to transport you to another place, another state of mind. In these times of rapid technological development and dizzying consumerism, cottage gardens evoke the perceived simplicity and idealism of a bygone age.

Big on colour and scent, cottage gardens are an assault on our senses; grasses, along with the buzzing of bees, bring sound into the equation.

I don't feel that it's necessary to give a suggested plant list in this section. Whatever your chosen colour scheme, there's a grass to enhance it. In a white garden, for example, *Carex oshimensis* 'Evergold' gives an intense creamy splash at the front of the border. *Miscanthus sinensis* 'Morning Light' has to be one of the most modest of grasses; its leaves are narrow and edged with soft white; its habit is neat and compact; its blooms (which only appear in a particularly long, hot summers) are relatively small for a miscanthus and resemble expensive silk tassels in the softest smoky pink. This is a plant too well bred to flop onto its neighbours.

In the hot border plant *Uncinia rubra* for its resilient, burnt-brown, evergreen foliage. This unusually coloured grass forms neat clumps but it will self-seed so adopt a relaxed attitude – somehow it always seems to spring up in a

LEFT *Stipa gigantea* stands proud amongst perennials in this lovely cottage garden at Wootens of Wenhaston, Suffolk. *S. gigantea* has an enviable, gauzy quality that catches the eye but doesn't shield other plants from view

wholly appropriate spot. *Panicum virgatum* 'Warrior' forms wonderful, swaying clumps and becomes increasingly tinged with wine-red as the season progresses. Its open flower panicles are the colour of a 1961 Bordeaux – and, for some, just as exciting. As autumn turns to winter, panicum blazes through clear, golden yellow and into oaty brown.

If cool colours are more your style, front a border with *Koeleria glauca*, a dense hummock-forming grass that shoots out a profusion of bolt-upright flower stems from its centre. *Panicum virgatum* 'Blue Tower' is a wonder of a grass. Its colour has to be seen to be believed – it simply glows with a metallic silver-blue and fades through the same vivid yellow as *P. virgatum* 'Warrior'.

Hystrix patula, with its distinctive seedheads that resemble a flattened ear of wheat, is stunning in a bold sweep near the back of the border. It forms rather a solid visual mass, so provides a resting place for the eye before it skips on to echinops, delphiniums and salvias.

ABOVE In this contemporary take on the cottage garden at Apple Court in Hampshire, *Deschampsia cespitosa* vies for attention with a wonderful metal sculpture. The artwork cleverly echoes the sparkler-like form of the deschampsia

ABOVE This border in a show garden designed by the author uses grasses, including molinia and panicum, to tie the bold perennial planting together

ABOVE The habit of this miscanthus fits perfectly with the loose, tumbling feel of a cottage garden. The spectacular, glowing gold molinia at the rear appears to be lit from within

PAINTING WITH GRASSES

Use grasses in the cottage garden as brush strokes to unify your planting. They sway in the breeze and provide a transient, gauzy backdrop. The subtle hues of grasses encourage your carefully chosen perennials to shine out, without themselves paling into insignificance. *Stipa gigantea* is a cottage garden star, flowering from midsummer and holding its seedheads well into autumn, when they jangle around in the slightest breath of air. Planted in the middle of the border, stipa provides respite from the carnival of colour. *S. gigantea* is bold enough to be planted singly; its smaller sibling, *S. tenuissima*, is no less stunning but reaches its full potential when planted in drifts – try threes or fives, those perennial magic numbers!

ABOVE **Team grasses with cottage garden favourites such as** *Kniphofia* **'Wrexham Buttercup', red (yellow!) hot poker...**

A WELCOME BREAK?

Die-hard cottage gardeners may disagree with me, but I feel that sometimes a break from all those flowers perversely and subconsciously serves to increase the viewer's appreciation of them. Grasses give the eye a bit of a rest, a pause before you move on to more showy blooms. They are no less stunning than herbaceous perennials but grasses do grab your attention in a more subtle way.

RIGHT **This throughly modern take on the cottage garden sees grasses playing a dominant part whilst flowering perennials are used as punctuation. Are the tables turning?**

ABOVE ...*Salvia viridis*, annual clary sage...

ABOVE ...**agapanthus**...

ABOVE ...and of course roses. This rich, velvety red one is *Rosa* 'Peter Beales'

BAMBOOS IN COTTAGE GARDENS

Does bamboo have a place in the cottage garden? My feeling is not in the traditional 'chocolate box' one. But a new wave of contemporary cottage gardens (for want of better terminology) is emerging. A style that appreciates, no, depends upon, the perennials so prevalent in traditional gardens, but also tastefully introduces plants that have become popular in more recent years.

Take care though! Try to create a garden that knows where it's going, that's tied together by strong design. I know how difficult it sometimes is as an enthusiastic gardener and plant-lover to exercise restraint. By all means appreciate a range of styles but don't try to include them all in one garden – what's informally known as 'car crash gardening'. The result is likely to be an unsatisfying hotch-potch of mismatched design snapshots, not a contemporary garden.

RIGHT The bamboo at the rear of this cottage certainly doesn't look out of place – the planting is rather restrained though, with not a rose in sight. Is this why it works?

SMALL SPACES

Whether your small space amounts to a courtyard, the petite garden of a new-build home, a balcony, terrace or even a window box, if you have a hankering for grasses and bamboos, you can accommodate them. With

ABOVE This diminutive show garden at Chelsea Flower Show is reminiscent of a courtyard garden. There's still space for plenty of plants, as well as a seating area, thanks to cleverly designed raised beds. Cyperus steals the show in the front bed, which is kept moist thanks to a concealed porous pipe

the careful selection of well-behaved varieties you can create a garden that's still exciting and full of movement. Choose plants with contrasting habits, leaf colours and textures to ensure the scene you paint has plenty of depth and interest.

It's easy to think that filling a small space with plants is only going to make it seem smaller, but this isn't always the case. If you are clever and use a critical eye you can create a sense of mystery and suspense. Partially hiding elements of the garden can make it seem larger because it isn't laid bare at first glance, it still has some secrets. Use screening of some kind, an archway, plants, or preferably a combination. Taller grasses and bamboos are perfect for creating a sense of mystery – you can see through them (in varying degrees, depending on the variety) but they give depth and substance.

Clothing your boundaries with plants can soften them and make them appear 'fuzzy around the edges', therefore pushing them visually backwards. If you are willing to go to the effort of installing an impenetrable root barrier to form a channel along one or more boundaries, consider planting a bamboo screen. It can be kept narrow and thinned if necessary. *Phyllostachys vivax* f. *aureocaulis* will stun all who see it with its astounding, bright yellow stems. These thick canes carry airy, grass-green foliage that offers light dappling rather than real shade. See also 'Container culture' on page 38.

MINIMALISM

Some gardeners frown on minimalism, expressing the view that if a person was really passionate about plants they would want to fill their garden with them. But a minimalist garden can throw a plant into the limelight and give all those who see it a chance to drink in its form without distraction, to fully appreciate its beauty in a way that they might not have, were it surrounded by other plants.

The ethos of minimalist design is to pare a space down to its simplest, most stylish form; a state in which every element is earning its keep and displaying its purity. All clutter and distraction is banished. In the minimalist garden, construction materials are used to produce clean lines and planting is unfussy and restrained. This makes it the ideal design genre to choose if you want to make a big style statement in a small space.

Bamboos and grasses are a minimalist's dream thanks to their strong, arresting forms. If a minimalist style really is for you, choose bamboos and grasses that have clean, neat habits, not ones that tend to sprawl over pathways and become unruly. Stick to a few carefully selected varieties and use them with conviction, planting blocks of the same variety to amplify its form. Remember the minimalist mantra, 'less is more'.

ABOVE **Fescues, such as this *Festuca glauca* 'Blaufuchs' (blue fox) are perfect in a minimalist scheme because they retain their neat, tight, mounded shape**

PROPORTIONS

If you can cope with height, but not spread, your options are open to many clump-forming grasses and bamboos. Check the eventual spread to see if it will be feasible to grow the variety you fancy. And there are usually some cunning tricks you can pull to make things work out in your favour. For example, while the popular bamboo *Phyllostachys nigra* will eventually grow to about 20ft (6m), its spread will be a very manageable 3ft 3in (1m). And it's perfectly acceptable to remove or subtly trim a portion of the taller canes to keep the height in check.

ABOVE *Calamagrostis* x *acutiflora* 'Karl Foerster' is ideal for a small garden – although it reaches 6ft (1.8m) when in flower, it has a very upright habit and its spread is just 2ft (60cm) at the most

Pretty much any clump-forming grass is suitable for a small space as long as the height isn't going to block precious light. Obviously don't choose *Arundo donax* or *Miscanthus* x *giganteus* unless you fancy making your small garden even smaller. But don't confine your choices to only low growing varieties – planting in a range of heights will bring plenty of interest and actually make your plot seem larger. A variety such as *Calamagrostis* x *acutiflora* 'Karl Foerster' is perfect for bringing height and movement to the small plot. It forms a neat clump of soft green foliage with a spread of just 2ft (60cm) and in midsummer bears tall, strong, upright stems of feathery flowers that reach up to 6ft (1.8m). *C.* x *acutiflora* 'Overdam' is a variegated variety that has a similar spread but reaches about 4ft (1.2m) in bloom. The flower stems of both varieties fade to buff but remain in place all winter to bring out-of-season interest.

Whichever grasses and bamboos you plant, if you ever feel a clump has become too large simply split it in the spring and replant a division. A friend will be sure to take the surplus off your hands.

CONTAINERS

Pots are useful design tools in a small garden but you must make them earn their keep. Choose containers and the plants to go in them very carefully. Use plants that you really love, that have strong forms, and that you will continue to enjoy in the long term. Don't skimp on quality or container size – in a small garden a well-proportioned pot is a major focal point, perhaps *the* focal point. And don't have too many pots – clutter will make your space seem smaller.

SMALL IS BEAUTIFUL

Be resourceful and don't let your spacially challenged garden get you down! Use containers, raised beds and window boxes to increase your growing area. Some grasses can

SCREEN DREAMS

If you love the look of lofty bamboos but really don't have a suitable spot for one, why not clothe one or more of your boundaries with bamboo screening? It's widely available, fairly inexpensive and simple to install. Screening provides a fantastic backdrop for more diminutive bamboos and grasses, and its subtle colour and smooth texture are great for lightening the mood. It also covers unsightly walls and fences a treat!

ABOVE **Or ask a friend for some canes next time they're thinning their bamboo. They can be fashioned into garden art of some kind or into a simple but very attractive fence, just like this one at Jardin Majorelle in Marrakech**

ABOVE **If you haven't the space for a living bamboo but love the tactile culms, why not erect bamboo screening?**

be grown in hanging baskets. Dwarf, running bamboos look very stylish planted in the cavity along the top of a sturdily constructed hollow wall to form an unusual hedge, as long as the root run is fairly deep. Try this with *Pleioblastus pygmaeus* 'Distichus' or 'Ramosissimus' – both can be trimmed into shape and don't mind being razed to the ground.

RIGHT **These pots, backed by a *Phyllostachys aureosulcata* f. *aureocaulis*, create a great focal point in a small garden. Painting them is a quirky way to give high impact on a low budget. And if you're not partial to agaves, just plant your pots up with grasses!**

SECTION TWO

LEFT Neat but impressive, *Miscanthus sinensis* 'Yakushima Dwarf' takes all the positive points of *M. sinensis* and presents them in miniature

TYPICAL PLANT
HARDINESS ZONES
FOR WESTERN EUROPE

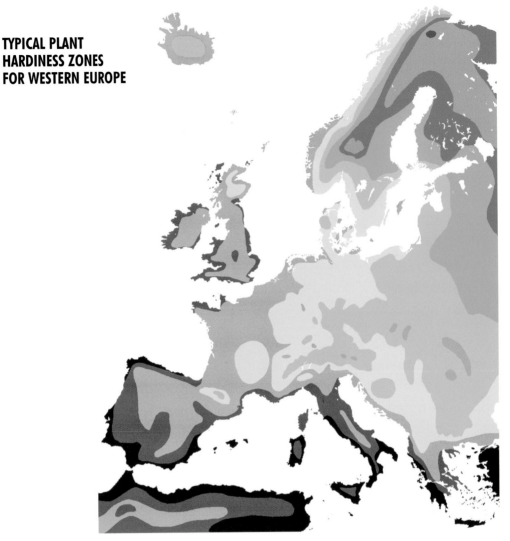

Grasses and bamboos grow naturally all over the world. A plant's natural origin has a huge bearing on its suitability for growing in different conditions under cultivation. That said, some plants are more adaptable than others and may, for example, tolerate temperatures considerably lower than those they are exposed to in the wild.

Bear in mind, too, that microclimates often exist within a garden. You may have an area that's a bit of a frost pocket or that is more exposed to the prevailing wind. Likewise, you may find that more tender bamboos and grasses will scrape through the winter unscathed if you plant them at the base of a warm, sunny wall.

Bamboos and grasses will develop a similar habit to that seen in nature if their cultivated conditions – light, temperature and moisture – are close to those in their natural habitat. Alter any one of these variables and the plant may still thrive, albeit with a different habit.

Remember that plants are adaptable – they want to grow. Use these maps to find bamboos and grasses that are hardy in your area. And if you fall for a plant that is too tender to overwinter outdoors don't be deterred, just bring it under cover over the winter. There is a solution to every problem; in fact, tricky situations often encourage resourcefulness and individuality.

**TYPICAL PLANT HARDINESS ZONES
FOR NORTH AMERICA**

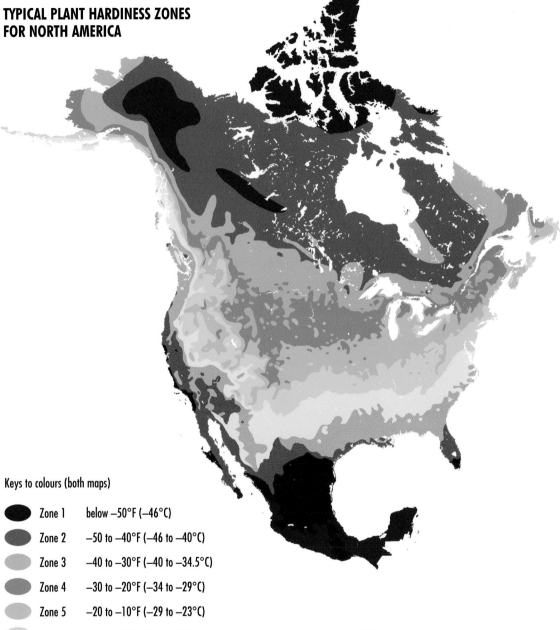

Keys to colours (both maps)

	Zone 1	below −50°F (−46°C)
	Zone 2	−50 to −40°F (−46 to −40°C)
	Zone 3	−40 to −30°F (−40 to −34.5°C)
	Zone 4	−30 to −20°F (−34 to −29°C)
	Zone 5	−20 to −10°F (−29 to −23°C)
	Zone 6	−10 to 0°F (−23 to −18°C)
	Zone 7	0 to 10°F (−18 to −12°C)
	Zone 8	10 to 20°F (−12 to −7°C)
	Zone 9	20 to 30°F (−7 to −1°C)
	Zone 10	30 to 40°F (−1 to 4°C)
	Zone 11	above 40°F (above 4°C)

HOW TO USE THESE MAPS

Each entry in the plant directory lists the relevant zones where it should
be possible to grow the plant successfully, based on these heat-zone
maps. Find your location on the map, and you can then identify the
zone that your area belongs to. Do not forget to take into account that
cities are warmer than rural locations. Planting shelter belts of trees and
shrubs or dividing the garden up with wind-calming screens can help to
give plants better conditions in which to thrive.

CHAPTER 5

A–Z plant directory

Within this directory are some of the most reliable, gardenworthy, not to mention beautiful, grasses and bamboos known to cultivation and available to the gardener. Some will greet you on a visit to any garden centre, whilst other little gems must be sought out from specialist nurseries. There are so many other varieties, species, forms and cultivars, but once you delve into the exciting world of bamboos and grasses, there's no doubt you'll become hooked and will make discoveries of your own. There would be no surprises for you at the nursery if everything was described here, would there? Use this directory as a starting point, be bold with your selections and make interesting combinations of colour, texture and form.

But remember not to think too deeply – some of the very best plant associations have been happy accidents. Bamboos and, to an even greater extent, grasses tone and tie schemes together. Their subtle colourations and shape-shifting forms mean that, come rain or shine, winter or summer, grasses and bamboos will continue to bring delight for seasons to come.

NOTE TO ENTRIES

'Notable species and varieties' refers to species, varieties, forms and cultivars. Where size and/or hardiness zone isn't mentioned, it is the same as the main entry. The size format is always height x spread.

NAME: *ARUNDO DONAX*

Type: Grass
USDA zone: Z6+
Description: Towering evergreen grass with sturdy, bamboo-like stems and broad, grey-green leaves. In cooler climes it will be knocked back by cold weather but will regrow in spring. There are noteworthy variegated varieties but these should be considered frost-tender; cut them back and move somewhere frost-free or leave them in situ and thoroughly cover with horticultural fleece.

In sheltered areas or particularly long, hot summers arundo will bear showy, pink-tinged, silvery flower plumes of 1ft (30cm) in height.

Height and spread: 15ft x 5ft (5m x 1.5m).
Where to grow: Best in sun or light shade on moist ground; however, arundo is very tolerant of a range of conditions and will cope with periods of drought. This statuesque grass makes a perfect backdrop to a tropical border, thanks to its bold foliage.
Maintenance: In cold areas, where foliage has browned over winter, cut all stems back to ground level in spring. This annual pruning will encourage larger leaves and can also be carried out in warmer areas where plants have remained evergreen. However, if flowers are favoured over bold foliage, just cut stems down every other year.

ABOVE **The bold foliage of *Arundo donax* is perfect for creating a tropical look**

Keep clumps in check by slicing through sections of the fleshy rhizome with a clean, sharp spade and discarding unwanted sections.

Propagation: Division or seed in spring. Keep young plants moist in a coldframe until large enough to pot on or plant out.

Notable species and varieties: *Arundo donax* var. *versicolor* has striking white variegation and is much smaller than the species – 6ft x 2ft (1.8m x 60cm).

A. *donax* 'Golden Chain' is acid yellow with narrow central stripes of green. Again, smaller and more manageable than the species.

NAME: *BRIZA MEDIA*

Type: Grass
USDA zone: Z4+
Description: Whilst the narrow, blue-green foliage of this perennial grass isn't much to get excited about, the delicate flower panicles are stunning. Borne in spring and lasting well into midsummer, they begin purplish and fade to straw colour. The slightest breeze makes them

ABOVE **This newly planted *Briza media* is already showing the flower panicles that earn it its common name of quaking grass**

ABOVE *Calamagrostis* x *acutiflora* 'Karl Foerster'

ABOVE The large, pale, drooping tassels of *Calamagrostis emodensis*

quiver and quake – hence the common name of quaking or trembling grass. Planted en masse, briza is quietly spectacular.

The blooming stems make lovely cut flowers and can be dried by hanging bunches upside down in a cool, dry, airy environment.

Height and spread: 3ft x 1ft (90 x 30cm).

Where to grow: Where not to grow may be more fitting! *Briza media* tolerates a broad spectrum of conditions from full sun to light or dappled shade on dry or moist, acid or alkaline soil. Will also tolerate heavy soils, despite its diminutive appearance.

Maintenance: Pretty as the flower panicles are, all that jiggling around takes its toll and by late summer plants appear rather dishevelled. Cut back the whole plant to remove the faded flower stems and encourage a fresh flush of foliage. The subsequent neat mound will provide autumn and winter interest.

Propagation: Allow seeds to dry and sow in autumn or the following spring. Divide in spring or early summer.

Notable species and varieties: *Briza maxima* may not quite attain the overall dimensions of *B. media* but its flowers are much larger and more showy. *B. minor* is the lesser quaking grass and is altogether more petite. Both these species are annuals.

B. media 'Russells' is a pretty, perennial, variegated but still strong-growing cultivar.

NAME: *CALAMAGROSTIS X ACUTIFLORA*

Type: Grass

USDA zone: Z4+

Description: This grass forms a clump of mid-green foliage which reaches its true potential when seen in drifts or mass plantings. But it's the flower spikes that are really stunning. The narrow inflorescences, held high on tightly arranged, poker-straight stems, appear in midsummer and last well into winter.

Height and spread: 6ft x 3ft (1.8m x 90cm).

Where to grow: Very tolerant of a range of conditions but prefers moist, fertile soil in full sun or light shade.

Maintenance: Leave the mounds of foliage and wonderful seedheads to provide long-lasting winter interest. As soon as new growth emerges in spring cut the whole plant to ground level.

Propagation: Divide in spring.

Notable species and varieties: *Calamagrostis* x *acutiflora* 'Karl Foerster' is deservedly the most widely grown cultivar. Its strongly upright stems carry sparkling silver-pink inflorescences. *C.* x *acutiflora* 'Overdam' is a very attractive variety with pink-flushed, creamy white variegation. The purplish blooms are held a little more loosely than the species.

C. *emodensis* has an altogether different habit, bearing wonderful drooping, cream-green tassels. *C. brachytricha* has a similar habit to *C.* x *acutiflora* but appears more robust with broader foliage and larger inflorescences of strongly purple-tinted flowers – beautiful.

NAME: CAREX

Type: Sedge

USDA zone: Various – see 'Notable species and varieties'.

Description: A huge genus covering all manner of foliage forms and colours, growth habits and cultivation requirements. There is a carex for every garden and many are also happy in containers; some are even suitable for growing at pond margins.

Height and spread: Various – see 'Notable species and varieties'.

Where to grow: All carex appreciate moisture, although some are tolerant of drier conditions. They will all thrive in sun or shade, though some prefer their shade on the light or dappled side. Let common sense prevail: more sun – more moisture; less sun – less moisture. And remember that those with variegation will remain pristine, as long as they are shielded from the scorching midday sun.

Maintenance: Cut deciduous varieties to the ground as new growth emerges in spring. Trim out faded blades of evergreen varieties throughout the warmer months.

Propagation: Divide in spring or early summer. Carex can be grown from seed. Less hardy varietes should be sown in spring and will need some warmth to aid germination, whereas those from cooler climes need exposure to cold so should be sown as soon as ripe and overwintered in a coldframe.

ABOVE **Lighting up a gloomy corner, this young *Carex* 'Ice Dance' is settling in nicely**

ABOVE This established swathe of *Carex siderosticha* 'Variegata' gives the feel of a body of flowing water as it carpets the ground. It is a slow spreader and easily kept within bounds

Notable species and varieties: *Carex buchananii* is an evergreen with very narrow, burnt orange foliage and an upright, fountain-like habit. 2½ft x 3ft (75 x 90cm). *C. comans* has a very similar habit but is a little smaller and can range in leaf colour from pale grey-green to rich chocolate brown. Also similar but usually with a more lax fountain habit and slightly longer, broader leaves is *C. flagillifera*. All Zone 7+.

C. testacea forms a fabulous robust mound of narrow, evergreen, burnt olive foliage. More fiery tones will be seen when grown in full sun.

Drought tolerant and suitable for containers. 2ft x 2ft (60cm x 60cm). Reaches up to 5ft (1.5m) when in flower but stems splay outwards rather than upwards. Zone 6+.

C. pendula can be invasive due to its exuberant attitude towards self-seeding. However, if you don't mind pulling out the (numerous) seedlings you'll be rewarded with an imposing evergreen sedge. Plentiful stems bear drooping flower spikes that resemble catkins. Very tolerant. 4½ft x 5ft (1.4m x 1.5m). Zone 7+.

C. elata 'Aurea' is in most grass-lovers' top ten for its arching foliage of intense gold or acid yellow. Plants are crowned in spring and early summer by erect stems, equally vibrant in colour to the leaves, topped by fuzzy brown flowers. Will grow at the water's edge. Foliage colour is strongest in spring; the shade will vary with light intensity. 2ft x 1½ft (60cm x 45cm). Zone 5+.

Some excellent variegated cultivars are: *C. phyllocephala* 'Sparkler' – very striking and unusual, thrives on moist soil or in shallow water (ideal for a mini pond in a watertight container). Tolerates full sun but light shade will prevent scorching. 2ft x 2ft (60cm x 60cm). Zone 8+.

C. 'Ice Dance' – a hardworking evergreen with broad, glossy, leathery, cream-edged leaves. Excellent singly or as groundcover when planted en masse. Can be cut back hard if it becomes shabby and will regrow strongly. 1ft x 1ft (30cm x 30cm). Zone 5+.

C. oshimensis 'Evergold' is a favourite; tough, narrow, evergreen leaves with an eye-catching, creamy yellow central stripe. Again, excellent planted in groups, but also great in a container where its leaves will droop over the edge of the pot. 1ft x 1ft (30cm x 30cm). Zone 6+.

C. siderosticha 'Variegata' – broad, fabulously bold foliage stays low to the ground and slowly spreads to form a dense carpet, without being invasive. Leaves are edged and streaked with white and give rise to spikes of brown flowers in spring. 1ft x 1½ft+ (30cm x 45cm+); height is less when not in flower. Zone 5+.

NAME: *CHASMANTHIUM LATIFOLIUM*

Type: Grass

USDA zone: Z5+

Description: Most grasses make some sort of rustling noise when the wind blows but *Chasmanthium latifolium* is something else. Its common name is spangle grass due to the unusual, almost diamond-shaped seedheads that rattle together in the breeze, making a dry, papery sound.

In a sunny spot the broad leaves are bright pale green and the stems grow narrowly upright; in shade the foliage is dark green and the whole plant adopts a more lax habit.

As the flowerheads dry out they turn from green through fiery shades, eventually becoming brown and splitting open. Autumn leaf colour is rich gold.

Height and spread: 3ft x 2ft (90cm x 60cm).

Where to grow: Very tolerant. Best in light or dappled shade but will cope admirably in full sun. Prefers moist, well-drained soil but will tolerate drought or poor drainage.

Maintenance: Cut all stems to ground level in late winter. Seedheads dry well – cut flowering stems in autumn before the seedheads split open and hang in bunches upside down in a cool, dry, airy spot.

Propagation: Divide in spring or early summer. Collect seed when ripe in the autumn and sow in spring.

Notable species and varieties: *Chasmanthium laxum* has an altogether more delicate appearance, although it will grow a little larger. The inflorescences are smaller and appear on stems that stand proud of the basal foliage. 5ft x 3ft (1.5m x 90cm). Zone 6+.

RIGHT **By early October the seedheads of this *Chasmanthium latifolium* are dry and they rattle together in the slightest breeze**

NAME: *CHIMONOBAMBUSA TUMIDISSINODA*

Type: Bamboo

USDA zone: Z7+

Description: For hundreds of years *Chimonobambusa tumidissinoda* has been used by craftsmen in China to make walking sticks. In a garden setting, despite its curiously swollen nodes made all the more prominent by a tan coloured band on every one, *C. tumidissinoda* somehow doesn't seem a showy or novelty plant. Quite the opposite in fact; its slender, elegantly arching canes and fans of narrow, bright green leaves bring a sense of grace and calm to the garden.

Height and spread: 13ft x 26ft (4m x 8m).

Where to grow: Light shade is best on moist fertile ground with protection from wind. Can be very invasive so only plant in open ground if you have plenty of space, otherwise grow in a large container. It will still fully develop its graceful habit but will be restricted in height (and obviously spread).

Maintenance: Thin out congested culms in spring to allow the remainder to be fully appreciated.

Propagation: Divide in spring.

Notable species and varieties: The variety *C. quadrangularis* has square stems that are particularly striking on older canes and close to the ground. Tolerates deep shade but must have shelter from wind to prevent it becoming very ragged looking. 13ft x 13ft (4m x 4m) or more in favourable conditions. Zone 7+.

C. marmorea has mottled new growth and fresh-looking, bright green foliage. 5ft x 10ft (1.5m x 3m). Zone 6+.

ABOVE *Chimonobambusa marmorea* sends forth its new growth late in the year – this specimen is seen at Kew Gardens in October

ABOVE The curious stems of *Chimonobambusa tumidissinoda* make this bamboo one of the most distinctive species

NAME: *CHUSQUEA CULEOU*

Type: Bamboo

USDA zone: Z8+

Description: A very variable species, one clone of *Chusquea culeou* can appear very different from the next. At its best it develops strong, stout, upright canes. The colouring can be bright yellow with prominent green nodes giving a stripy appearance, but it may be quite different from this. The papery sheaths clothing young stems add to the beauty of this bamboo.

Height and spread: 20ft x 4ft (6m x 1.2m).

Where to grow: Full sun or dappled shade on moist, well-drained soil that's rich in organic matter. Protect from cold winds.

Maintenance: Raise the canopy as desired to expose culms and thin out congested growth.

Propagation: Divide in spring and replant sections of rooted rhizome.

Notable species and varieties: *C. gigantea* is a fine, large species that stands up to strong sunlight, wind and salt-laden air. Its stout canes develop flushes of red and orange as they age. 33ft x 13ft (10m x 4m). Zone 6+.

ABOVE The culms of *Chusquea culeou* are so striking – some with papery sheaths, some showing dramatic yellow and green stripes

ABOVE *Chusquea culeou* has many guises and one specimen may be wildly different from another

ABOVE More compact than the species, and with fine creamy variegation, *Cortaderia selloana* 'Albolineata' makes a statement in the mixed border or as a specimen plant

ABOVE With its elegantly drooping plumes, *Cortaderia richardii* is a more graceful take on *C. selloana*

NAME: *CORTADERIA SELLOANA*

Type: Grass
USDA zone: Z9+
Description: Often the victim of overplanting, *Cortaderia selloana* (pampas grass) fell out of favour but is thankfully undergoing a revival thanks to more tasteful placement and the introduction of compact cultivars. For drama and height in the mixed or grass border, cortaderia, an evergreen, can't be beaten. It's shimmering plumes catch the light and stand for many months on strong stems.
Height and spread: 8ft x 5ft (2.5m x 1.5m).
Where to grow: Well-drained soil in full sun.

Maintenance: Wearing thick, gauntlet-style gloves as protection from the razor-sharp leaves, trim or comb out dead foliage in early spring to make way for fresh growth. Also at this time use secateurs to cut out flower stems left for winter interest.

Young plants may need protection through their first couple of winters, so protect them with a thick layer of horticultural fleece.
Propagation: Divide in spring.
Notable species and varieties: The excellent *C. selloana* 'Sunningdale Silver' is reliable and readily available. Its silver plumes stand up to wind and rain even better than the species.

'Pumila' is also easy to get hold of. It has shimmering yellow flower plumes and is more compact – 5ft x 4ft (1.5m x 1.2m).

Pink-plumed varieties to look out for are 'Pink Feather' and 'Candyfloss'. If you fancy a bit of variegation try cool, creamy 'Albolineata' or gold 'Aureolineata'. 'Splendid Star' and 'Cool Ice' are variegated and dwarf – perfect for a pot.

If all these showy plumes aren't your style, seek out *C. richardii*. It has all the robust qualities of *C. selloana* but its flowerheads resemble gracefully arching feathers as its stems fan outwards. Prefers a little more moisture than *C. selloana* – fantastic by water. Zone 8+.

NAME: *CYPERUS PAPYRUS*

Type: Sedge
USDA zone: Z9+
Description: *Cyperus papyrus* is the original sedge used to make paper in ancient Egypt. Today its globes of filament-like bracts on tall, strong, leafless stems bring exoticism to any water garden.
Height and spread: 6ft x 3ft (1.8m x 90cm).
Where to grow: Prefers full sun but will tolerate light shade. For the lushest, healthiest growth make sure the soil is kept moist, or better still, plant in a basket of aquatic compost and submerse at the pond margin.
Maintenance: Keep the soil moist, especially through the growing season. In frost-prone areas plants should be moved into a bright, frost-free greenhouse over winter. Tidy up dead growth in spring.
Propagation: Divide in spring. Also in spring try sowing seed collected the previous autumn. Use ordinary seed compost but ensure that it remains constantly moist.
Notable species and varieties: *C. involucratus* has wider, much more leaf-like bracts. It is often grown as a house plant. 2½ft x 2½ft (75cm x 75cm). Zone 8+.

C. eragrostis is shorter, hardier and less showy but makes a talking point nonetheless.

It has plenty of basal leaves and pom-pom inflorescences of pale green flowers. Self-seeds freely and doesn't require the high moisture levels that most other species do. 3 x 1½ft (90 x 45cm). Zone 6+.

ABOVE **The threadlike bracts of *Cyperus papyrus* bear small, brown flowers and become longer and more lax with age**

NAME: *DESCHAMPSIA CESPITOSA*

Type: Grass

USDA zone: Z4+

Description: A hardy evergreen, *Deschampsia cespitosa* is a great grass for a wide range of garden situations. The leaves are mid-green and fairly unremarkable, but form such pleasing, neat mounds that a drift of *D. cespitosa* is very satisfying to behold. When they flower, the billowing clouds of shimmering buff-coloured blooms create a haze above the tidy foliage.

Height and spread: 4ft x 3ft (1.2m x 90cm).

Where to grow: Very tolerant of a wide range of light and moisture levels and it will grow happily on an acid or alkaline plot.

Maintenance: In spring trim out faded flower stems left for winter interest and also remove any dead leaves.

Propagation: Divide in spring or early summer. Sow seed in spring or autumn.

Notable species and varieties: *D. cespitosa* 'Goldtau' is deservedly the most widely grown cultivar. It's neater, more compact and even prettier. The delicate inflorescences are a glimmering yellow. 2ft x 2ft (60cm x 60cm). 'Bronzeschleier' is a little taller than 'Goldtau' and its inflorescences are shiny bronze.

D. flexuosa 'Tatra Gold' is fantastic at best, but a little bit scrappy at worst. It forms neat mounds of very fine, acid-yellow foliage, from the centre of

ABOVE **At Apple Court in Hampshire the bleached stems and seedheads of** *Deschampsia cespitosa* **'Goldtau' dance in the autumn light**

ABOVE **In July the bronze tinted inflorescences of *Deschampsia cespitosa* 'Bronzeschleier' shimmer and sparkle in the sunlight**

which emerges a dense clump of yellow stems, which support panicles of bronze flowers. Excellent en masse. Dead foliage tends to appear around the edge of the plant and so you should gently tug this away to make way for fresh growth. 1½ft × 1ft (45cm × 30cm).

NAME: *FARGESIA NITIDA*

Type: Bamboo
USDA zone: Z5+
Description: *Fargesia nitida* is quite a variable species so one clone may look very different to another. Apart from this, growing conditions have quite an influence on appearance.

Whatever its growing conditions or parentage, *F. nitida* tends to adopt a graceful, fountain-like habit. Thanks to its very slender canes it is widely used in China for weaving and basket making.
Height and spread: 10ft × 3ft (3m × 90cm).

ABOVE **The fine foliage and fountain-like habit of *Fargesia nitida* makes it a distinctive bamboo**

Where to grow: Moist but well-drained soil. Tolerant of a range of conditions but culms will change colour depending on light levels.

Light shade will encourage dark canes whilst avoiding leaf scorch. However, the canes will become still darker in bright light but be aware that a percentage of foliage may be damaged by strong sunlight. *F. nitida* will also tolerate deep shade but growth may be less vigorous and culms will be an unremarkable green.

Maintenance: Little maintenance is needed. Thin canes if necessary.

Propagation: Divide in spring or early summer.

Notable species and varieties: *F. murielae* forms a dense fountain and is extremely hardy, suitable for cold, exposed situations. New canes are bright green, yellowing with age. 13ft x 10ft (4m x 3m).

F. fungosa has a bolder look than other fargesias thanks to its larger leaves. Its stems flush red with age. 13ft x 4ft (4m x 1.2m). Zone 7+.

F. denudata has yellow canes (particularly in full sun) and yellow-green leaves. Again, it has a dense, urn-like habit but can be quite open and floppy when young. 13ft x 3ft (4m x 90cm). Zone 6+.

ABOVE *Fargesia denudata* can be rather sparse and weeping when young but will soon become strongly upright

NAME: *FESTUCA GLAUCA*

Type: Grass

USDA zone: Z4+

Description: Tough and evergreen, *Festuca glauca*, or blue fescue, stands out among grasses for its neat, dense mounds of narrow foliage that seems to glow icy grey-blue. It bears plumes of flowers of the same distinctive blue colour during summer. By autumn these stems will have dried to straw yellow.

Height and spread: 1ft x 1ft (30cm x 30cm).

Where to grow: Develops the strongest colouring in full sun. Will tolerate poor, dry soil. Very easy to please.

Maintenance: Trim out faded flower stems as they become tatty, usually in autumn.

If you wish to maintain that glowing blue foliage it's necessary to divide plants every three years to encourage vigorous new growth. It is this juvenile foliage that shows the strongest colouration.

Propagation: Divide in spring. Sow seed when ripe in autumn through to spring.

Notable species and varieties: *F. glauca* 'Elijah Blue' is widely available and very reliable. Has more of a silver-grey tint than the species.

The foliage of *F. glauca* 'Blaufuchs' (blue fox) is intensely blue while *F. glauca* 'Golden Toupee' is more compact and has fresh, bright, soft yellow-green leaves.

F. amethystina has super-fine, sea-green foliage that flops beautifully – but not untidily. Its flowers are borne on the slenderest of stems that are often flushed red and arc outwards in a feathery fountain.

RIGHT *Festuca glauca* 'Elijah Blue' is one of the most popular fescues for its steely blue foliage and arching flower stems in midsummer

NAME: *HAKONECHLOA MACRA 'AUREOLA'*

Type: Grass

USDA zone: Z4+

Description: A drift of *Hakonechloa macra* 'Aureola' will light up the gloomiest corner with its sprays of weeping, bright yellow, green-streaked leaves. Masses of sparkler-like flowers are borne in late summer but they are subtle, not showy, and simply enhance the quiet beauty of this grass. Foliage becomes flushed with red tones in autumn (or if hungry!) and this is a glorious sight.

Height and spread: 16in x 16in (40cm x 40cm).

Where to grow: Best in dappled or light shade but will tolerate full sun or deeper shade. Will produce the most luxurient growth on moist, well-drained soil that's rich in organic matter. Also grows well in a pot.

Maintenance: Trim to ground level in spring before new growth emerges. If a hakonechloa needs moving, do it in spring rather than autumn.

Propagation: Divide in spring.

Notable species and varieties: *H. macra* 'Albovariegata' is more subtly variegated; its leaves are predominently mid- to dark matt green with cream streaks. *H. macra* 'All Gold' is just what it says on the label! May scorch in strong sunlight so provide some shade.

ABOVE Graceful *Hakonechloa macra* 'Aureola' demands attention without being a show-off and is perfect for lending a Japanese feel to the garden

ABOVE *Helictotrichon sempervirens* is a fine grass for a coastal or roadside garden thanks to the protective waxy coating on its leaves

NAME: *HELICTOTRICHON SEMPERVIRENS*

Type: Grass

USDA zone: Z4+

Description: *Helictotrichon sempervirens* is a tough grass and can stand up to salt-laden or polluted air. It forms a tight, spiky mound of blue-grey foliage that's topped with fans of flowers in springtime, drying oat-colour and lasting well through summer.

Height and spread: 4 x 2ft (1.2m x 60cm).

Where to grow: Full sun and well-drained soil. Good in pots and looks amazing in casual drifts or arranged in a contemporary, geometric style.

Maintenance: Trim out faded flower stems in late summer.

Propagation: Divide or sow seed in spring.

Notable species and varieties: The foliage of *H. sempervirens* 'Saphirsprudel' is even bluer.

131

NAME: *HIBANOBAMBUSA TRANQUILLANS*

Type: Bamboo

USDA zone: Z6+

Description: Its really big, shiny leaves make *Hibanobambusa tranquillans* a distinctive and gardenworthy bamboo. When mature it forms a dense, rounded clump – very pleasing!

Height and spread: 13ft x 10ft (4m x 3m).

Where to grow: Tolerates dry ground but tends to grow more quickly as it searches for water. Prefers full sun or light shade.

Maintenance: Thin out congested culms as necessary in early spring.

Propagation: Divide in spring.

Notable species and varieties: *H. tranquillans* 'Shiroshima' is the bamboo to plant if you're after a brightly variegated, reliable variety. It even remains strongly variegated in shade, which is a welcome but uncommon trait. 10ft x 5ft (3m x 1.5m).

NAME: *IMPERATA CYLINDRICA* 'RUBRA'

Type: Grass

USDA zone: Z7+ or a little cooler

Description: Unmatched in the red-leaf stakes, *Imperata cylindrica* 'Rubra', often called 'Red Baron', is a lowish, spreading grass that, when planted en masse, creates rivers of fire through a border. Its broad blades grow bolt upright and are bright green at the bases with a punchy red flush that starts at the tip and works its way down as the season progresses.

ABOVE **An excellent variegated bamboo,** *Hibanobambusa tranquillans* 'Shiroshima' **keeps its creamy striations even in shade**

ABOVE **Even in October, as it begins to die back, *Imperata cylindrica* 'Rubra' glows with vibrancy**

Height and spread: 16in x 16in (40cm x 40cm).
Where to grow: Can be slow to spread but will get off to the best start on moist, well-drained soil, rich in organic matter. Position it where it will be backlit by the sun – the whole plant will appear aflame.

Maintenance: Provide a light, dry winter mulch through the first couple of years.
Propagation: Divide in spring or summer.

133

NAME: *JUNCUS PATENS*

Type: Rush

USDA zone: Z6+

Description: *Juncus patens* is similar to the common rush *J. effusus* but is more compact and rigid in habit. *J. patens* also has more of a bluey cast to its stiff, hollow stems – like most other juncus, it lacks leaves. Fuzzy clusters of brown flowers appear close to the stem tips throughout summer. In cooler areas juncus dries to straw colour; in warmer climes it remains evergreen.

Height and spread: 2ft x 2ft (60cm x 60cm).

Where to grow: Grows best in full sun or light shade. Prefers moist soil and will grow at pond margins. Also good in pots if kept moist – stand in a saucer of water.

Maintenance: Little needed. Tidy up as necessary.

Propagation: Divide in spring or early summer. Sow seed in spring.

Notable species and varieties: *J. patens* 'Carman's Gray' is a popular cultivar with

ABOVE The stiffly upright *Juncus patens* 'Elk Blue' punctuates the border and is especially effective planted in drifts

ABOVE **By autumn the flower stems of _Koeleria vallesiana_ have bleached but are still very attractive**

greyish blue-green stems, whilst _J. patens_ 'Elk Blue' has a strong glaucous blue tint.

J. effusus f. _spiralis, J. decipens_ 'Curly Wurly' and _J. inflexus_ 'Afro' are all variations on a curly-stemmed theme – always a talking point and especially popular with children. Because their stems are twisted, plants are more compact and sometimes form a dense, snake-like mat.

NAME: _KOELERIA GLAUCA_

Type: Grass
USDA zone: Z6+
Description: Another fine blue grass, _Koeleria glauca_ thrives on poor, shallow soil in full sun. It forms a compact mound, from the centre of which spring masses of erect stems, each topped with a cylinder of shimmering, silvery

green flowers. As these stems age and the seeds ripen they bleach and contrast beautifully with the bluey grey-green foliage.
Height and spread: 1½ft x 1ft (45cm x 30cm).
Where to grow: Needs full sun and fairly low nutrient levels. Tolerates a range of conditions from moist but well-drained through to dry. Happiest on poor, chalky or sandy soil so perfect for a coastal garden.
Maintenance: Remove flower stems as they become untidy and trim out dead leaves in early spring.
Propagation: Divide or sow seed in spring.
Notable species and varieties: _K. vallesiana_ has a very similar habit but is slightly larger and more sea green than blue-grey.

ABOVE Don't you just want to touch them? The fluffy seedheads of *Lagurus ovatus* have earned this grass the common name of bunny's tails

NAME: *LAGURUS OVATUS*

Type: Grass
USDA zone: Z6+
Description: This annual grass is grown for its wonderful fluffy flowerheads which are produced in abundance over a long period through the summer. They begin pale green with a purplish cast and dry to straw colour.
Height and spread: 1 ½ft x 1ft (45cm x 30cm).
Where to grow: Full sun and fertile, preferably sandy, free-draining soil.
Maintenance: Cut stems for drying before the seeds have fully ripened – when they are still tinged with green. Hang upside down in bunches in a cool, dry, airy position.
Propagation: Sow seed outdoors in spring. Alternatively start off in pots in a coldframe or cool greenhouse in autumn.

NAME: *LEYMUS RACEMOSUS*

Type: Grass
USDA zone: Z6+
Description: Often confused with *Leymus arenarius*, one of the grasses seen growing on sand dunes, *L. racemosus* is smaller and less rampant, though by no means less impressive. Its leaves are an undeniable steely blue-grey and they seem to burst forth in explosive fountains of shimmering silver.
Height and spread: 4ft x 4ft+ (1.2m x 1.2m+).
Where to grow: Full sun and well-drained soil.
Maintenance: Cut to ground level in autumn once growth has become tatty or in early spring.
Propagation: Divide in spring or summer.

NAME: *MISCANTHUS SINENSIS*

Type: Grass
USDA zone: Z6+
Description: If there's a genus that grass lovers become obsessed with it's miscanthus. In a dizzying array of leaf and plume colours, as well as different sizes, there's a miscanthus for every garden. Look out for jazzily variegated cultivars and those with rich purple plumes.

ABOVE **Fountains of silvery blades make *Leymus racemosus* a bold, eye-catching grass for a large border or informal, coastal-style planting**

Height and spread: Various – see 'Notable species and varieties'.

Where to grow: Miscanthus are very tolerant but you'll get the best from them if they're grown in full sun on moist but well-drained, fertile soil. Don't plant miscanthus in areas that suffer from excessive winter wet.

Maintenance: Leave stems and seedheads over winter to provide interest and snacks for birds. Cut down to ground level in early spring.

Propagation: Divide in spring. Divisions may be slow to establish so pot them up and grow on in a greenhouse or coldframe until plenty of healthy root can be seen.

Notable species and varieties: *Miscanthus sinensis* 'Cabaret' is one of the most stunning variegated cultivars, with creamy white-striped leaves. 6ft x 4ft (1.8m x 1.2m).

M. sinensis 'Morning Light' is shy to flower but more than makes up for this with its refined, silvery variegation, often touched with pink or purple. 4ft x 3ft (1.2m x 90cm).

ABOVE **Large, bold striped leaves make *Miscanthus sinensis* 'Cabaret' one of the most sought-after cultivars**

137

M. sinensis 'Strictus', 'Zebrinus', 'Little Zebra' and 'Gold Bar' are variegated cultivars with horizontal gold banding. The leaves of 'Zebrinus' can be quite long and lax but the other three are dense and compact and have strongly upright, almost spiky foliage.

M. sinensis 'Ferner Osten' is a gorgeous one with deep red-purple, open flower panicles above narrow, arching foliage. 6ft x 4ft (1.8m x 1.2m).

M. sinensis 'Little Kitten' is a compact cultivar with silver-beige flower panicles above narrow foliage. 4ft x 3ft (1.2m x 90cm).

Look out for introductions from Ernest Pagels, such as 'Malepartus', 'Nippon', 'Kleine Silberspinne' – a good nurseryman will know what you're talking about! There are many, many excellent miscanthus – too many to mention here. Just dive in and start exploring!

ABOVE **Simply beautiful, the sparse panicles of *Miscanthus sinensis* 'Ferner Osten' emerge shimmering purple and become silver-pink as they elongate and mature**

ABOVE *Miscanthus sinensis* 'Yakushima Dwarf' forms a dense mound that becomes entirely covered in neat, silvery plumes by late summer

ABOVE The fine foliage of *Miscanthus sinensis* 'Kleine Silberspinne' gives rise to masses of pink-tinged, silvery flower panicles. Here, as the seeds ripen in late autumn, the panicles have matured to buff colour

ABOVE As autumn sets in, *Molinia caerulea* subsp. *arundinacea* 'Skyracer' develops wonderful clear yellow tones to its stems, seedheads and foliage

NAME: *MOLINIA CAERULEA*

Type: Grass

USDA zone: Z4+

Description: Molinias are among the most beautiful and graceful of all grasses. Whilst their foliage is usually unremarkable – matt, mid-green – when they flower in midsummer, molinias send out the most wonderful arching sprays of sparkler-like panicles that sway and swell on the breeze. And that modest, green foliage becomes clear, bright yellow with the onset of autumn.

Height and spread: 5ft x 1½ft (1.5m x 45cm).

Where to grow: Full sun or semi-shade. Prefers acid – neutral soil (pH7 or below) and moist, well-drained conditions.

Maintenance: Cut to ground level in spring just before new growth appears. Leave flower stems over winter but trim out if they become untidy.

Propagation: Divide or sow seed in spring.

ABOVE It's midsummer at Knoll Gardens, Dorset, and *Molinia caerulea* subsp. *arundinacea* 'Karl Foerster' is in full flower

Whichever method you choose, do it in pots and keep the young plants in a coldframe until established.

Notable species and varieties: *Molinia caerulea* subsp. *caerulea* 'Edith Dudszus' is stunning against a pale backdrop – its flower panicles are deep purple on dark stems. 3ft x 1½ft (90cm x 45cm).

M. caerulea subsp. *arundinacea* 'Skyracer' is tall. Flower stems tend to grow upright before arching as they age. 6½ft x 2ft (2m x 60cm).

The variety *M. caerulea* subsp. *arundinacea* 'Transparent' is also tall, with very slender flower stems. The seedheads are open sprays – very beautiful. 6ft x 1½ft (1.8m x 45cm).

M. caerulea subsp. *caerulea* 'Variegata' is compact and forms a pleasing mound of yellow and green-striped foliage. Flower stems are golden yellow and flowers are purple. 1½ft x 1½ft (45cm x 45cm).

NAME: *PANICUM VIRGATUM*

Type: Grass
USDA zone: Z4+
Description: Another plant that no grass-lover should be without is panicum. It has many positive attributes: a tidy, upright habit that gently fans out towards the top; a range of exciting leaf colours from blue to burgundy; good autumn colour; shimmering panicles of flowers (often dark red) over a long period; the list goes on. To find out how fabulous they are you'll have to grow a few and see for yourself!
Height and spread: 4ft x 2½ft (1.2m x 75cm).
Where to grow: Easy going and tolerant. Best in sun and well-drained soil.
Maintenance: Leave the whole plant to give winter interest, then cut to the ground in spring or earlier if it becomes tatty.
Propagation: Divide or sow seed in spring.
Notable species and varieties: *Panicum virgatum* 'Heavy Metal' is an excellent, reliable, bluish cultivar with a neat, upright habit. 4ft x 2½ft (1.2m x 75cm).

ABOVE **This *Panicum virgatum* 'Rubrum' shows the fiery autumn colours typical of switch grass**

The variety *P. virgatum* 'Shenandoah' has the best deep red foliage and a dense, tidy habit. 3ft x 2ft (90cm x 75cm).

P. virgatum 'Blue Tower' stands apart from (and above!) other blue-leaved panicums with its amazing column of arching, wide, pale blue-grey leaves. 8ft x 3ft (2.4m x 90cm).

Another excellent, tallish cultivar is *P. virgatum* 'Cloud Nine'. Its foliage is bluish and the masses of airy flower panicles are shimmering gold. Foliage and seedheads turn deep golden yellow in autumn. 6½ft x 3ft (2m x 90cm).

Readily available and thoroughly reliable, the varieties *P. virgatum* 'Warrior', 'Squaw' and 'Rotstrahbusch' are also highly recommended.

ABOVE **An immense plant,** *Panicum virgatum* **'Blue Tower' is seen here in midsummer, about to burst forth into flower**

NAME: PENNISETUM

Type: Grass

USDA zone: Various – see 'Notable species and varieties'.

Description: There's no denying it – these are the fluffiest, most touchy-feely flowerheads in the grass world. They come in a huge array of shapes, colours and sizes from greenish white, though soft pink, to almost black.

Height and spread: Various – see 'Notable species and varieties'.

Where to grow: Full sun and moist but well-drained soil is essential. Winter wet will not be tolerated.

Maintenance: Leave foliage and seedheads in place over winter to provide bird treats and interest. The seedheads of hardy varieties look stunning with a dusting of frost – be sure to cover frost-tender varieties with a thick layer of horticultural fleece in cold and/or wet weather.

Cut the whole plant to ground level as the new growth appears in spring.

Propagation: Divide once strong growth has started in late spring or early summer.

Notable species and varieties: *Pennisetum orientale* 'Karley Rose' is a fabulous cultivar, taller than the species, with deep pink, long, fluffy flowerheads. 4ft x 2½ft (1.2m x 75cm). Zone 6+.

P. thunbergii 'Red Buttons' is a cheeky-looking plant with super-thin flower stems, each topped with a little fluffy flowerhead. Flowers start bright, deep red and turn beige as the seeds ripen. 3ft x 2ft (90cm x 60cm). Zone 7+.

For an explosion of feisty foliage and dramatic, drooping flowers it's hard to beat *P. setaceum* 'Rubrum'. Although it isn't hardy, it's worth fussing over this pennisetum and bringing it somewhere frost-free over winter. 5ft x 2ft (1.5m x 60cm). Zone 8+.

P. macrourum looks like a firework display when it's in bloom, with its long, dense, buff-coloured panicles on arching stems above a mound of bright green foliage. 6ft x 4ft (1.8m x 1.2m).

ABOVE ***Pennisetum orientale* looks good from a distance but get close up to really appreciate these gorgeous, fluffy seedheads**

For an intense hit of purple-black, grow annual *Pennisetum glaucum* 'Purple Majesty' from seed and plant out after the danger of frost has passed.

P. alopecuroides 'Hameln' and 'Little Bunny' are both widely available, compact and very attractive with incredibly fluffy flowers. 2ft x 2ft (60cm x 60cm) and 1ft x 1ft (30cm x 30cm) respectively. Zone 6+.

ABOVE Slender and plentiful, the culms of *Phyllostachys humilis* will form a lovely grove in time

NAME: PHYLLOSTACHYS

Type: Bamboo

USDA zone: Z6+ unless otherwise stated

Description: Phyllostachys is the genus most widely available for sale by a long shot. It contains many important species such as *Phyllostachys nigra*, *P. aurea*, *P. aureosulcata* and *P. bambusoides* to name but a few.

For the most part phyllostachys is easy to grow, gardenworthy and rewarding. Many species have been grown in China for hundreds of years and used for construction, in food, as utensils, canes, fishing rods and much more.

They may exhibit vastly differing growth habits depending on the temperature, light and moisture levels in your locality but it is worth noting that phyllostachys are some of the most cold-tolerant bamboos. In colder conditions they will form tight, neat, manageable clumps and although most will still grow tall – over 13ft (4m) – they will not reach their full potential height. In warmer climes however, phyllostachys species will quickly spread, the culms emerging further apart to give a bamboo forest effect. They will also show off their admirable stature, some reaching up to 40ft (12m). But don't fear – there is a phyllostachys for every situation.

Height and spread: Various – see 'Notable species and varieties'.

Where to grow: Various conditions are preferred or tolerated but as a general rule, sun or light, dappled shade and moist but well-drained soil will keep most phyllostachys happy.

Maintenance: Thin culms as necessary in early spring to let light and fresh air amongst the canes and to show them off at their best.

Propagation: Divide in spring.

Notable species and varieties: There are many, many excellent species, forms and cultivars and this is by no means an exhaustive list of all gardenworthy plants. A visit to a specialist nursery is the best way to get to grips with this large and wonderful genus and to see for yourself all it has to offer. Look out for:

P. aurea 'Holochrysa' – bright yellow canes. 13ft x 5ft (4m x 1.5m). Zone 5+.

P. aureosulcata – curious wiggly canes, excellent overall habit. 20ft x 8ft (6m x 2.5m).

P. aureosulcata f. *spectabilis* – golden yellow, flushed red and green. 20ft x 8ft (6m x 2.5m). Zone 5+.

P. bambusoides 'Allgold' – wonderful, smooth, rich yellow canes. 20ft x 8ft (6m x 2.5m). Zone 7+.

P. flexuosa – arching, slender, green, zig-zag canes with contrasting coral-coloured sheaths. 16ft x 6ft (5m x 1.8m).

P. nigra – slim, black stems emerge green and darken with age. 20ft x 5ft (6m x 1.5m).

P. violascens – yellow, green and purple striped, flushed canes. 30ft x 10ft (10m x 3m).

P. vivax f. *aureocaulis* – absolutely stunning, thick, golden yellow canes with green stripes and prominent nodes. 30ft x 10ft (10m x 3m).

ABOVE **The culms of *Phyllostachys nigra* 'Boryana' are heavily blotched with dark purple-brown. As for habit, it's a very variable cultivar**

ABOVE *Pleioblastus argentiostriatus* f. *glaber* is bright and fresh-leaved and makes excellent, well-behaved groundcover

NAME: PLEIOBLASTUS

Type: Bamboo

USDA zone: Z6+ unless otherwise stated

Description: The genus pleioblastus has within it many vibrantly variegated dwarf bamboos that are perfectly suitable as groundcover, in pots and as informal hedging.

Not all are dwarf though; in fact some reach 13ft (4m) or higher. However, you can be sure with pleioblastus that, regardless of height, the foliage will be very special.

Height and spread: Various – see 'Notable species and varieties'.

Where to grow: Easy going – sun or shade on moist, but preferably well-drained soil.

Maintenance: Dwarf varieties can be mown to the ground annually during the latter part of winter. Plenty of fresh new growth will appear over the subsequent few weeks.

Propagation: Divide in spring.

Notable species and varieties: *P. argenteo-striatus* has several fine variegated forms and cultivars including 'Akebono', 'Okinadake', f. *glaber* and f. *pumilus*. All are dwarf and form dense mounds or clumps, rather than romping away, devouring all in their paths. Zone 7+.

P. linearis is a tall variety and forms a neat clump of graceful, slightly arching stems. It has very attractive long, drooping leaves. 13ft x 6ft (4m x 1.8m).

P. pygmaeus spreads rapidly under ideal conditions and makes a perfect, dense carpet under taller bamboos or trees, or alongside a pathway. The leaves have a very distinctive arrangement and the edges often become bleached to pale beige during the winter. 1ft x 13ft (30cm x 4m). Zone 4+.

P. simonii is an excellent clump-forming bamboo. The leaves are slender and the stems very straight and upright. Thin out the canes regularly to show this bamboo in its best light. Use the prunings as plant supports. 13ft x 5ft (4m x 1.5m). Zone 5+.

A vibrant species with bright acid-yellow and green-striped leaves, P. viridistriatus is deservedly popular. 4ft x 6ft (1.2m x 1.8m). Zone 5+.

ABOVE *Pleioblastus viridistriatus* will bring a splash of acid-bright colour to a dull corner in dappled, light or half-day shade

ABOVE For a distinctly different bamboo choose *Pleioblastus linearis* for its long, drooping, bright green leaves on arching canes

ABOVE **With its strong, vertical lines and large leaves, *Pseudosasa amabilis* has a very individual look**

NAME: *PSEUDOSASA AMABILIS*

Type: Bamboo

USDA zone: Z8+

Description: Whilst *Pseudosasa amabilis* will rarely exhibit mature characteristics in a British garden, it will still cut a dash with its rigidly upright habit. The culms are clothed in pale buff-coloured sheaths, which means that they contrast really well with the bright green foliage.

Height and spread: 20ft x 5ft (6m x 1.5m).

Where to grow: In a sheltered spot in sun or dappled shade. Moist but well-drained soil.

Maintenance: Cut out oldest culms annually – they make excellent garden canes, or fishing rods for that matter!

Propagation: Divide in spring.

Notable species and varieties: *P. japonica* is very easy to grow and highly attractive. Like *P. amabilis*, it has a strongly upright habit but it's far more hardy. 13ft x 10ft (4m x 3m). Zone 5.

NAME: SASA

Type: Bamboo

USDA zone: Z4+

Description: Sasas are hardy, architectural plants that clothe the ground with their bold foliage held on the slenderest of culms. Some can be highly invasive but others are far more controllable. They are suitable for pot culture and can also be mown to the ground at the end of each winter to produce the freshest new growth every spring.

A characteristic of most sasas is that their leaf margins bleach with the onset of cold weather. This should not be considered a defect – it gives an attractive variegated appearance and these damaged leaves can simply be sheared off before new growth commences. Or, if left in place they will quickly be disguised by the new season's stems.

Height and spread: Various – see 'Notable species and varieties'.

Where to grow: Very tolerant – will cope admirably with light levels ranging from full sun

ABOVE **The subtlety of variegation gives *Sasa kurilensis* 'Shira-shimofuri' a beautiful, silvery appearance**

ABOVE **Said to be superior to the species, *Sasa veitchii* f. *minor* forms a dense carpet of these fantasic big leaves**

to deep shade and moisture levels from damp to dry. Make sure the ground is on the moist side if planting in full sun. Dry shade may encourage a tighter, better-behaved clump.

Maintenance: After winter remove any leaves that have become very shabby. Also at this time thin out culms as necessary.

Propagation: Divide in spring.

Notable species and varieties: Unusually variegated *Sasa kurilensis* 'Shira-shimofuri' can be trusted to behave itself. It is far less rampant than the species and even though it's variegated it will make itself at home in fairly deep shade. 6ft x 10ft (1.8m x 3m).

S. palmata f. *nebulosa* has wonderful, bold, palm-like foliage but it can be very invasive so plant with care and be prepared to chop out unwelcome new growth annually. A more prudent option would be to grow it in a large container. This bamboo creates a fabulous tropical effect with its deeply veined, oversized leaves – thin culms annually to get the best look. 6½ft x 16ft (2m x 5m).

S. nipponica and *S. veitchii* f. *minor* both show winter bleaching on pretty much every leaf, giving a spectacular show. *S. nipponica* hugs the ground, reaching 1ft x 10ft (30cm x 3m) and should be mown each winter for the best foliage. *S. veitchii* f. *minor* grows to 3ft x 10ft (90cm x 3m) and it can also be sheared to the ground.

NAME: *SEMIARUNDINARIA FASTUOSA*

Type: Bamboo
USDA zone: Z5+
Description: *Semiarundinaria fastuosa* forms a great column of strong, stout, strictly upright culms. The overall effect is bright green, punctuated by the large, pale, papery culm sheaths – a real sight to behold.
Height and spread: 23ft x 8ft (7m x 2.5m).
Where to grow: Very tough and tolerant of dry or damp soil. Cold hardy and will still perform excellently on exposed sites and in coastal conditions. Have to put up with inner city air

ABOVE *Semiarundinaria lubrica* forms a neat clump – get up close and personal to enjoy the finer details of this subtle plant

ABOVE What an impressive bamboo! The culms of *Semiarundinaria fastuosa* are amazingly vertical and clothed at every node in these papery sheaths

ABOVE **This dense stand of** *Semiarundinaria kagamiana* **is in need of judicious thinning to better show off the distinctive form. It creates just the right mood in a Japanese garden**

pollution? Put this bamboo on your shopping list!
Maintenance: In early spring thin culms if necessary and remove any unwanted growth.
Propagation: Divide in spring.
Notable species and varieties: *Semiarundinaria yashadake* f. *kimmei* is a really lovely plant with a very distinctive form. Its stems are particularly slim and they splay out in a fountain shape, topped by fresh green foliage. 10ft x 6ft (3m x 1.8m). Zone 6+.

Semiarundinaria kagamiana is reminiscent of Japanese ink drawings with its slightly leaning stems of splayed, bright green leaves, held almost horizontally. 13ft x 6½ft (4m x 2m). Zone 6+.

NAME: *SHIBATAEA KUMASACA*

Type: Bamboo

USDA zone: Z5+

Description: *Shibataea kumasaca* is a small, neat, rounded bamboo with short, pointed, spoon-shaped leaves. Up close you'll see that its very slim culms are deep red, contrasting perfectly with the bright green foliage.

S. *kumasaca* makes a great potted specimen and performs impeccably in the garden too. Its leaves become bleached at the margins in winter.

Height and spread: 3ft x 3ft (90cm x 90cm) or a little more.

Where to grow: Will grow in full sun or light shade but needs reliably moist soil in sun.

Maintenance: Thin out culms in early spring to reduce overcrowding and better appreciate the form of this bamboo.

Propagation: Divide in spring.

Notable species and varieties: S. *chinensis* is similar to S. *kumasaca* but is a little smaller and will happily grow on clay or chalky alkaline soil.

ABOVE **Deliciously different, *Shibataea kumasaca* is a wonderful bamboo for a tight spot or a pot**

NAME: *STIPA GIGANTEA*

Type: Bamboo

USDA zone: Z5+

Description: *Stipa gigantea* is a king among grasses. It is tall and stately yet utterly transparent; evergreen and architectural; easy to grow and as wonderful as a single specimen as it is in a bold drift. With a mound of narrow, mid-green leaves and an eruption of strong golden stems, topped with waving, whispering seedheads, *S. gigantea* will transform a sunny spot into something special.

Height and spread: 6½ft x 4ft (2m x 1.2m) or a touch taller.

Where to grow: Plant in full sun and well-drained soil. An easy, impressive grass.

Maintenance: Trim out faded flower stems as they become shabby. Also clip out dead foliage. Be aware that stipas are shallow rooting – if you move a clump don't be alarmed by the lack of abundant roots, just make sure it's firmed well into its new position.

Propagation: Collect and dry seed in autumn, then sow in spring. Divide late spring or early summer.

Notable species and varieties: *S. gigantea* 'Gold Fontaene' is an excellent cultivar, overall slightly larger and even more eye-catching.

S. tenuissima creates a fountain of very fine foliage and flower stems that start bright green and become pale blonde as the season wears on. Despite this delicacy, *S. tenuissima* rarely becomes scruffy, even over winter, and is a truly delightful addition to a sunny garden. Plant in drifts for best effect. 2ft x 1ft (60cm x 30cm).

S. calamagrostis is a lovely variety. It bears clouds of feathery, shimmering flower panicles that droop gently above sea-green foliage. 3ft x 4ft (90cm x 1.2m).

RIGHT **One of the most splendid grasses of all –** ***Stipa gigantea*** **or giant oats**

NAME: *THAMNOCALAMUS CRASSINODUS*

Type: Bamboo

USDA zone: Z7+

Description: If you're looking for an elegant bamboo, maybe something a little different, look no further than *Thamnocalamus crassinodus*. It forms a distinct clump of strong, upright culms that have a beautiful, waxy, pale blue coating when juvenile. The long, narrow, soft blue-green leaves cascade down from the main culms on slim, pink-tinged stems.

Height and spread: 13ft x 4ft (4m x 1.2m).

Where to grow: Prefers light or dappled shade and moist, well-drained soil. Shelter from the wind.

Maintenance: Thin in spring as necessary.

Propagation: Divide in early spring – with varying degrees of success!

Notable species and varieties: *Thamnocalamus crassinodus* 'Kew Beauty' is a wonder of a bamboo, exhibiting a rainbow of colours in its smooth, straight culms. The young culms emerge with a pale blue-grey, waxy coating, then mature through rich beige, finally becoming bright, deep red, sometimes tinged purple. 13ft x 4ft (4m x 1.2m).

T. crassinodus 'Lang Tang' has tiny, bright green leaves that create a lovely, lacy effect. 10ft x 3ft (3m x 90cm).

ABOVE **The elegant, weeping habit of** *Thamnocalamus crassinodus* **makes it a fine specimen bamboo**

ABOVE **A cascade of fine foliage awaits the fortunate keeper of** *Yushania anceps*

NAME: *YUSHANIA ANCEPS*

Type: Bamboo
USDA zone: Z5+
Description: A variable but always elegant bamboo. Its tall, straight culms have very widely spaced nodes – a distinctive characteristic – and they arch considerably, showing off the long, particularly narrow leaves beautifully.
Height and spread: 13ft x 6½ft (4m x 2m), sometimes taller.

Where to grow: Tolerant of a range of conditions but prefers sun and moist, well-drained soil.
Maintenance: Thin out culms as necessary in early spring.
Propagation: Divide in spring.
Notable species and varieties: *Y. maculata* has slender, olive-green culms with distinctive dark brown sheaths when juvenile. Bright, deep green foliage hangs enticingly like long fingers. 13ft x 6½ft (4m x 2m).

Glossary

Annual

A plant that completes its life cycle in one year.

Culm

Above ground stem.

Glaucous

The blue, grey, white or silvery appearance given by a coating or 'bloom' on leaves and stems. Often seen on plants native to coastal regions.

Hardiness

A plant's ability to withstand cold temperatures. Plants can usually tolerate very short periods at slightly lower than desirable temperatures. Gradual acclimatization to lowest tolerated temperatures is always recommended. Tender: tolerates temperatures down to 5°C (41°F). Half hardy: tolerates temperatures down to 0°C (32°F). Frost hardy: tolerates temperatures down to −5°C (23°F). Fully hardy: tolerates temperatures down to −15°C (5°F).

Herbaceous

A plant whose above-ground parts die at the end of the growing season. If not cut back these stems and seedheads become desiccated and can provide winter interest. Meanwhile the roots remain alive below ground and send up new shoots in spring.

Inflorescence

Flower arrangement on a stem, for example panicle, spike, raceme, umbel.

Internode

The space (stem) between nodes.

Leptomorph

A bamboo with a spreading habit.

Loam

Soil composed of roughly equal measures of sand, silt and clay. Loam is free draining but moisture retentive and usually has good nutrient levels. It's easy to work and its structure remains stable over time.

Node

Point on a stem from which growth (leaves and new stems) arises. Nodes are often swollen and/or a different colour to the rest of the stem.

pH

Used to indicate the acidity or alkalinity of a substance. pH 7 is neutral, below is acid and above is alkaline. Garden soil is said to be neutral at pH6.5 and usually ranges between 5.5 and 7.5.

Pachymorph

A bamboo with a clump-forming habit.

Perennial

A plant that takes three or more years to complete its life cycle. Most perennials will live for many more than three years before they begin to decline of natural causes.

Rhizome

Fleshy, horizontal-growing, usually underground stem that acts as a storage organ and gives rise to roots.

Sheath

Material that covers and protects emerging new growth. On bamboos the culm sheaths are often very noticeable, especially as they turn pale and papery as they dry out.

Stolon

Stem that grows across the soil surface and sends out roots, so increasing the spread of a plant (often aggressively) and forming new plantlets.

Stomata

Pores in the leaves and stems of plants that allow gaseous exchange – 'plant breathing'.

Variegated

Foliage that lacks chlorophyll in certain areas. This gives decorative white or yellow colouration, usually around the leaf margin or in stripes, but bands and spots are also seen.

About the author

Lucinda Costello is a gardening writer based in Dorset on the south coast of England. One of the reasons she lives here is the favourable climate that allows her to grow a wonderful range of plants, including tender varieties, outdoors all year round.

Lucinda trained in horticulture and garden design at Pershore College of Horticulture in the Cotswolds. While still training, she worked with many times RHS Gold Medal-winning nursery, Rushfields of Ledbury, at Chelsea, Hampton Court, Tatton Park and Birmingham NEC flower shows. After graduating Lucinda spent several years working at G-Scapes of Lichfield, a nursery and landscaping business. She took time out to travel the world with her partner Robert and on her return, she began her first journalism job as gardening writer at *Amateur Gardening* magazine, successfully combining her love of plants, writing and photography. During her time there, Lucinda designed a show garden that went on to win Large Gold and Best in Show.

Lucinda now writes and assists Robert – who owns a successful garden design and landscaping business – with designs and planting schemes. Her love of colour and form frequently spills over into other disciplines and she is currently exploring textile art, with flowers and foliage as the inspiration for much of her work.

Index

Photographs of plants are indicated by page numbers in **bold**.

GMC Publications Ltd, 166 High Street, Lewes, East Sussex BN7 1XU, United Kingdom
Tel: 01273 488005 Fax: 01273 402866
www.gmcbooks.com

Contact us for a complete catalogue, or visit our website.